NATIONAL DEFENSE RESEARCH INSTITUTE

T0306491

RISK FACTORS FOR SEXUAL ASSAULT AND SEXUAL HARASSMENT IN THE U.S. MILITARY

Findings from the 2014 RAND Military Workplace Study

Terry L. Schell, Andrew R. Morral, Matthew Cefalu,

Coreen Farris, Miriam Matthews

Prepared for the DoD Sexual Assault Prevention and Response Office

For more information on this publication, visit www.rand.org/t/RR870z9

Library of Congress Cataloging-in-Publication Data is available for this publication.
ISBN: 978-1-9774-0316-2

Published by the RAND Corporation, Santa Monica, Calif.
© Copyright 2021 RAND Corporation
RAND® is a registered trademark.

Support RAND
Make a tax-deductible charitable contribution at
www.rand.org/giving/contribute

www.rand.org

Preface

The Sexual Assault Prevention and Response Office within the Office of the Secretary of Defense selected the RAND Corporation to provide a new and independent evaluation of sexual assault, sexual harassment, and gender discrimination across the U.S. military. The U.S. Department of Defense (DoD) asked the RAND research team to redesign the approach used in previous DoD surveys, if changes would improve the accuracy and validity of the survey results for estimating the prevalence of sexual crimes and violations. In the summer of 2014, RAND fielded a new survey as part of the RAND Military Workplace Study.

This report describes survey data analyses designed to identify characteristics of service members and of the environments in which members work that are associated with each individual's risk of sexual assault or sexual harassment. The series that collectively describes the study methodology and its findings, to date, includes the following reports:

- *Sexual Assault and Sexual Harassment in the U.S. Military: Top-Line Estimates for Active-Duty Service Members from the 2014 RAND Military Workplace Study*
- *Sexual Assault and Sexual Harassment in the U.S. Military: Top-Line Estimates for Active-Duty Coast Guard Members from the 2014 RAND Military Workplace Study*
- *Sexual Assault and Sexual Harassment in the U.S. Military: Volume 1. Design of the 2014 RAND Military Workplace Study*
- *Sexual Assault and Sexual Harassment in the U.S. Military: Volume 2. Estimates for Department of Defense Service Members from the 2014 RAND Military Workplace Study*
- *Sexual Assault and Sexual Harassment in the U.S. Military: Annex to Volume 2. Tabular Results from the 2014 RAND Military Workplace Study for Department of Defense Service Members*
- *Sexual Assault and Sexual Harassment in the U.S. Military: Volume 3. Estimates for Coast Guard Service Members from the 2014 RAND Military Workplace Study*
- *Sexual Assault and Sexual Harassment in the U.S. Military: Annex to Volume 3. Tabular Results from the 2014 RAND Military Workplace Study for Coast Guard Service Members*

- *Sexual Assault and Sexual Harassment in the U.S. Military: Volume 4. Investigations of Potential Bias in Estimates from the 2014 RAND Military Workplace Study*
- *Sexual Assault and Sexual Harassment in the U.S. Military: Volume 5. Estimates for Installation- and Command-Level Risk of Sexual Assault and Sexual Harassment from the 2014 RAND Military Workplace Study*
- *Sexual Assault and Sexual Harassment in the U.S. Military: Annex to Volume 5. Tabular Results from the 2014 RAND Military Workplace Study for Installation- and Command-Level Risk of Sexual Assault and Sexual Harassment*
- *Risk Factors for Sexual Assault and Sexual Harassment in the U.S. Military: Findings from the 2014 RAND Military Workplace Study*
- *Effects of Sexual Assault and Sexual Harassment on Separation from the U.S. Military: Findings from the 2014 RAND Military Workplace Study.*

These reports are available online at www.rand.org/surveys/rmws.

The research reported here was completed in July 2018 and underwent security review with the sponsor and the Defense Office of Prepublication and Security Review before public release.

This research was sponsored by the U.S. Department of Defense and conducted within the Forces and Resources Policy Center of the RAND National Security Research Division (NSRD), which operates the National Defense Research Institute (NDRI), a federally funded research and development center sponsored by the Office of the Secretary of Defense, the Joint Staff, the Unified Combatant Commands, the Navy, the Marine Corps, the defense agencies, and the defense intelligence enterprise.

For more information on the Forces and Resources Policy Center, see www.rand.org/nsrd/frp or contact the director (contact information is provided on the webpage).

Contents

Tables

Summary

In this report, we identify risk factors for sexual assault and sexual harassment that may be useful to military leaders as they seek to improve prevention and response efforts.[1] Our goal was to produce interpretable estimates for the role of each potential factor in explaining risk of sexual assault and sexual harassment. To do so, we built a progressive series of multivariate models that accounted for known or logical relationships among the various predictors. For instance, age and rank are highly correlated, and both are significantly associated with sexual assault risk. Therefore, we treated age as conceptually prior to rank; that is, a person's age might affect his or her rank, but rank cannot affect age. We built the multivariate models in steps, beginning with demographic factors determined at birth, then adding characteristics determined before entering the military, then stable military characteristics, and then experiences in the past year. When investigating the role of each group of risk factors, we control for the preceding sets.

By examining how much each factor explains risk over and above what can be explained by conceptually prior factors, the analysis provides a more interpretable picture of the role of each risk factor. This information could be helpful in efforts to better target prevention interventions. Factors that are correlated with risk but explain very little of it after controlling for conceptually prior factors are likely to be poor targets for risk-reduction interventions. Conversely, factors that predict risk even after controlling for conceptually prior factors may deserve special consideration in prevention and training efforts.

Literature Review and Candidate Risk Factors for Analysis

Prior research has identified some risk factors associated with sexual assault and sexual harassment in civilian or military populations. For example, women, both civilians and those in the military, are more likely than men to be sexually assaulted or sexually

---

[1] The U.S. Department of Defense (DoD) requires that the following statement be included in this report: Reference to sexual assault is based on survey respondents' answers to questions about their experiences but does not reflect whether a sexual assault was substantiated by an investigation. Use of the terms *perpetrator* and *victim* in this report are not intended to presume the guilt or innocence of an individual.

harassed. In addition, the risk of sexual assault and sexual harassment appears to be higher for younger adults compared with older adults and for those who are single or divorced compared with those who are married. Results addressing the extent to which race is associated with sexual assault risk are inconsistent, and the association between race and sexual harassment among those in the military is complex. Lower academic performance appears to be associated with sexual assault victimization, and lower educational attainment is associated with increased risk of sexual harassment.

When we focus on military characteristics, prior research shows that service members in the Air Force are at lower risk of sexual assault and sexual harassment than those in other services are. Overall, enlisted service members are at higher risk of sexual assault and sexual harassment than officers are. Within these groups, the risk of sexual assault and harassment is higher for junior enlisted compared with more-senior enlisted service members and for junior officers compared with senior officers. Initial research suggests that, when military work groups are disproportionately male, there might be a greater risk of sexual assault and sexual harassment for those in the work group. In addition, research has suggested that women who combat deploy are at increased risk of combined sexual assault and sexual harassment. Risk of sexual assault and sexual harassment may differ by occupation in the military; for instance, combat specialists appear to face higher risks than health care specialists do.

Finally, research suggests a strong association between recent sexual assault experiences and earlier sexual assault experiences. This association could arise from several possible mechanisms, each of which might have different implications for preventing sexual assault. However, the existing literature does not currently clarify which mechanisms are most likely.

Although the literature review identified many factors associated with sexual assault and sexual harassment, this research often has examined a small number of potential risk factors, assessed self-reported risk factors, or involved analyses that exclude important known risk factors. In each case, the resulting associations could provide a misleading picture of the factors and characteristics that are most important for understanding sexual assault and sexual harassment risk. Our analyses included the risk factors identified via literature review and others and systematically assessed the effects of candidate risk factors in a conceptually guided series of models. The approach helped distinguish between correlations that appear to be unique to specific risk factors and those that are explained by theoretically preexisting factors.

Study Data

The data used for our analyses included administrative data provided by the Defense Manpower Data Center (DMDC) and survey data collected as part of the 2014 RAND Military Workplace Study (RMWS). The RMWS survey was one of the largest surveys of its kind: A representative sample of almost 560,000 active-duty and reserve-component service members were invited to participate, and more than 170,000 completed the web-administered survey. Although the RMWS includes a small number of respondents from the reserve component and the Coast Guard, the present analyses focus exclusively on results from active-duty members of the four DoD services.

The RMWS sampled 100 percent of active-duty women and 25 percent of active-duty men in the DoD services. Within gender groups, personnel were sampled with equal probability. Given differences in the survey version that service members were randomly assigned to receive, sample sizes for the risk models differed. For the sexual assault risk models described in this report, we used information on past-year sexual assaults from 115,759 active-duty service members (62,161 men and 53,598 women), and for the sexual harassment risk models, we used information on past-year sexual harassment from 65,539 active-duty service members (35,443 men and 30,096 women).

Approach to Estimating the Effect Sizes Associated with Risk Factors for Sexual Assault and Sexual Harassment

We wish to assess the extent to which various factors, including individual characteristics and military service factors, may be important predictors of risk of sexual assault and sexual harassment. This can be a challenge in our case because some of the factors of interest are known to influence other factors. For example, the importance of age in determining sexual assault risk may occur, in part, via the known and strong causal effect of age on rank in the military. Thus, one would not want to control for rank if trying to estimate the overall importance of age. Such a model would underestimate the importance of age because part of the total effect of age is mediated through another factor in the model. On the other hand, when trying to assess the importance of rank, one should control for age. This is because age could create a spurious bivariate association between sexual assault and rank by having causal effects on both. For our purposes, it would be inappropriate to throw all of the factors into a "kitchen sink" model. In such a model, effects for some factors would represent only the direct component of the effect conditioned on specific mediators, while effects for other factors may represent the total effect of the factor. This would make it difficult to interpret comparisons of the magnitude of the estimated effects across factors.

To avoid these interpretational problems, we used an approach sometimes referred to as *sequential multiple regression* (e.g., Cohen et al., 2002; Tabachnick and Fidell, 2007). In this approach, variables that are thought to temporally or causally precede other variables are entered in a sequence of models earlier than variables that are plausibly influenced by the early variables. In this study, we sorted the candidate predictors (i.e., the risk factors) into four ordered classes (*tiers*) corresponding to their temporal or conceptual priority: (1) birth demographics, (2) characteristics at the time of service entry, (3) personal and career history characteristics, and (4) recent experiences. For factors in each tier, we estimated their effects while controlling for the factors in earlier tiers. Thus, we estimated the importance of the risk factors assuming that factors in later tiers might be influenced by factors in earlier tiers and that factors in earlier tiers were unlikely to be affected by those in later tiers.

Our general analytic approach, therefore, was to predict the prevalence of sexual assault and sexual harassment from a series of regression models that sequentially add later tiers of risk factors. For each set of regressions, we report the bivariate association of factors in the tier with risk (one factor at a time) and show how factors in the tier singly and cumulatively improve upon a model consisting only of factors from the conceptually prior tiers. All models were run separately for women and men.

We examined the strength of the association between factors in two ways. First, we calculated relative risk ratios for service members with a particular characteristic (or factor value) compared with service members without the characteristic. This is an effect size estimate that explains how much the characteristic is associated with risk for members with the characteristic. But a characteristic or factor value associated with a very high relative risk might not explain a lot of sexual assault risk across the military if very few members have the characteristic. Therefore, we also estimated effect sizes at the population level by assessing how much that factor improves our overall ability to identify those who were and were not sexually assaulted. This was done by comparing the average model-predicted probability of assault for those who were assaulted to the average for those who were not. This measure varies between zero and one. A model that has no predictors would give the same predicted probability of assault for both groups, for a difference of zero. A model that perfectly predicts assault would have predicted probabilities of one and zero for the two groups, for a difference of one. Using this metric, we can determine the extent to which a given risk factor improves our ability to predict sexual assault throughout the military.

Sexual Assault Risk Among Service Women

An estimated 4.9 percent of service women were sexually assaulted in the year prior to the administration of the RMWS survey. This base rate of risk could be further differentiated using women's age and race, which were significantly associated with sexual assault risk. Specifically, being older in age and being white rather than Asian, black, or Hispanic was associated with elevated risk. However, age accounted for a greater proportion of the difference in risk between assaulted and nonassaulted service women than did race. Together, these birth demographics accounted for approximately a 1.5–percentage point difference in risk between the two groups. Specifically, using the model that included age and race, the average predicted probability among women who were sexually assaulted was approximately 6.2 percent, while the average predicted probability among women who were not sexually assaulted was 4.8 percent.

When we considered characteristics at the time of service entry, service women who indicated having experiences consistent with sexual assault prior to joining the military had a substantially elevated risk of sexual assault in the past 12 months. In addition, having higher scores on the Armed Forces Qualification Test (AFQT); serving in the Army, Navy, or Marine Corps; and being an enlisted service member (rather than an officer) were all associated with increased sexual assault risk. As a whole, factors known at the time of service entry accounted for an additional 3.5–percentage point difference in risk between assaulted and nonassaulted service women beyond that accounted for by birth demographics, which made factors at entry the tier of factors that contributed most to the prediction of women's sexual assault.

Service women's personal history characteristics—namely, being single, having fewer dependents, and having never attended college—were also associated with increased risk of sexual assault across all assessed models. In addition, risk for women appeared to be significantly higher in some occupational groups, with the lowest rates found for service women in the health care fields. Personal and career history factors accounted for little additional risk differentiation beyond that explained by birth demographics and characteristics at entry.

When we considered factors that described recent (past-year) experiences, service women who were deployed, served overseas, or served on a ship were all more likely to have been sexually assaulted in the past year than women without those experiences. However, when accounting for conceptually prior factors, serving overseas was no longer a significant predictor of risk, and the effect of serving on a ship was substantially attenuated.

Among the organizational characteristics of the units where service women served, having a higher proportion of men in the organization was associated with elevated risk in certain models. Model results showed that women who left the military recently were more than twice as likely to have been sexually assaulted than women who remained in the military were. Like personal and career history characteristics, recent experiences did less to differentiate between assaulted and nonassaulted groups of service women than birth demographics and characteristics at entry did, when controlling for those earlier factors.

Sexual Assault Risk Among Service Men

When we analyzed results for service men, age, but not race, was significantly associated with sexual assault risk. As seen with service women, service men who reported experiences consistent with sexual assault prior to joining the military were at substantially elevated risk of being sexually assaulted in the past year. Military service branch and entry type (enlisted, officer from a service academy, officer from the Reserve Officers' Training Corps [ROTC], other officer) were additional characteristics at the time of service entry that significantly predicted sexual assault risk in the multivariate model that included both birth demographics and all other characteristics at entry. Although an estimated 0.9 percent of all active-duty service men in DoD were sexually assaulted in the past year, the predicted risk of sexual assault from a model including characteristics at entry averaged 3.8 percent for men who experienced a sexual assault in the past year and 0.9 percent for those who did not. This is a substantial improvement in risk differentiation compared with the model that included only birth demographics.

For service men, being single and having few dependents were the only personal history factors associated with elevated sexual assault risk that significantly improved upon the model with birth demographics and characteristics at entry. Among career history factors, only pay grade significantly improved upon the model. Specifically, men in E1–E4 pay grades had the highest risk of sexual assault. As seen with service women, when controlling for birth demographics and characteristics at entry, personal and career history factors provided only a small improvement in risk differentiation between assaulted and nonassaulted service men.

Serving overseas in the past year, which was associated with elevated sexual assault risk, was the only recent experience factor that significantly predicted risk when controlling for all prior tiers, but it was not significantly associated with risk after accounting for the correlated factors of being deployed or serving on a ship. In addition, the risk of having been sexually assaulted in the past year was almost five times higher for men who left the military recently than for men who remained in the military. Adding recent experiences to the model modestly improved the ability to differentiate between assaulted and nonassaulted service men, providing a 1.2–percentage point improvement over the model that included all previously considered characteristics and experiences. These recent experiences may be somewhat more important predictors of risk for men than for women.

Sexual Harassment Risk Among Service Women

Knowing nothing about service women's individual risk factors, we would be unable to distinguish the risk of those who experienced sexual harassment in the past year and those who did not. We would assume that both groups have the DoD average risk of approximately 21.6 percent. Using a model that included age and race, the predicted risk of sexual harassment averaged approximately 23.3 percent for women who experienced sexual harassment in the past year and 21.1 percent for those who did not. Age accounted for most of this differentiation, with younger women being at higher risk of sexual harassment.

Including characteristics at the time of service entry in the model identified several additional predictors. Higher AFQT scores among enlisted women were associated with elevated risk of sexual harassment. Furthermore, women classified as having experienced a sexual assault prior to joining the military had a much higher risk of past-year sexual harassment. Branch of service was also a strong predictor of harassment risk, with women in the Air Force having lower risk than those in the other services. Adding characteristics at entry to the model improved the risk differentiation between harassed and nonharassed service women by 5.6 percentage points over the model that contained demographics only.

Among personal and career history factors, being single and having lower educational attainment each predicted elevated risk, and the model with these factors provided significant improvements over the model that included birth demographics and characteristics at entry only. But the effects of being single and attaining lower levels of education on sexual harassment risk were relatively small. Pay grade was also a significant predictor: E4 service members had a significantly higher risk of sexual harassment than all other pay grades besides the O1–O3 group. Among career history factors, occupational group provided the greatest improvement in prediction of risk over conceptually prior factors. Overall, personal and career history factors improved upon differentiation of harassed and nonharassed women by 1.16 percentage points over the prior model.

When we added recent (past-year) experiences to the model, service on a ship was significantly associated with increased risk of sexual harassment. Among the organizational factors that described service women's workplace in the past year, only percentage male was consistently a significant predictor of elevated risk across all levels of organization units (i.e., unit, installation, and major command). Finally, women who had separated from the service in the past year were at higher risk of having also been sexually harassed in the past year than were women who remained in the service. Adding recent experiences to the model improved the differentiation between sexually harassed and nonharassed women by 1.05 percentage points over the previous model.

Sexual Harassment Risk Among Service Men

When we analyzed results for service men, birth demographics were significant predictors of sexual harassment risk, but unlike analyses of service women's risk, neither age nor race strongly differentiated harassed and nonharassed service men. On average, an estimated 6.6 percent of DoD active-component service men experienced sexual harassment in the year prior to the survey. The predicted risk of sexual harassment from a model that included only birth demographics averaged approximately 7.3 percent for men who experienced sexual harassment in the past year and 6.6 percent for those who did not. This represents a quite small 0.66–percentage point differentiation in risk for this model.

When predicting sexual harassment risk among service men, many of the associations for characteristics known at entry were similar to those found when predicting risk among service women. For example, having higher AFQT scores was positively associated with sexual harassment risk; experiencing sexual assault prior to joining the military increased risk of sexual harassment during the past year of military service; and harassment risk was lowest among members of the Air Force. Service men who entered as officers had 0.6 to 0.7 times the risk of sexual harassment as service men who entered as enlisted. Overall, characteristics at entry improved differentiation of risk between harassed and nonharassed men by an additional 2.3 percentage points over the model that included only birth demographics.

No personal history factors were strongly associated with sexual harassment against service men after controlling for birth demographics and characteristics at entry. However, pay grade was a significant predictor among the career history factors and explained a substantial portion of population risk; men in the E4 pay grade had the highest risk of past-year sexual harassment. Years of deployment had a small but statistically significant inverse association with risk, and some occupational groups had significantly higher risk than others. Personal and career history factors improved risk differentiation between harassed and nonharassed service men by 1.52 percentage points over a model that included only birth demographics and characteristics at entry.

When we incorporated recent experiences into the analysis, serving on a ship in the past year was significantly associated with elevated risk. Working with younger service members, a higher proportion of men, and in places with larger numbers of service members were all organizational characteristics associated with elevated risk in all or most organizational groupings (unit, installation, and major command) when controlling for predictors from the earlier tiers. When controlling for all previously entered factors, men who separated from the military were 2.3 times more likely to have been sexually harassed in the past year than those who did not separate.

The Common Set of Risk Factors

One of the striking findings across the four different sets of models we estimated was the similarity in the effect sizes across genders and across sexual assault and sexual harassment outcomes. We quantified the similarity in the pattern of effect sizes by examining the correlation between model coefficients across the four models. The model coefficients that predicted sexual assault risk were strongly correlated ($r = 0.77$) with the analogous coefficients predicting sexual harassment across both women and men. Similarly, the model coefficients for women were strongly correlated ($r = 0.71$) with the analogous coefficients for men, across both sexual assault and sexual harassment. Given this similarity in the effects across models, it is probably useful to think about a common set of risk factors for both women and men and for both sexual assault and sexual harassment.

Although there was considerable similarity in the effect sizes, there were also a few notable differences across the models. Experiencing pre-service sexual assault, being older, and being single all showed more-extreme risk ratios with sexual assault than with sexual harassment. Race was one of the few factors for which the effects changed direction across women and men. White men were generally at lower risk for sexual assault and harassment than other racial groups were, whereas white women were generally at higher risk than other racial groups were.

Unmeasured Risk Factors

Although the final risk models for sexual assault and sexual harassment provided insight into many factors associated with risk, there is still considerable uncertainty about who will be assaulted and who will not. Some of the remaining uncertainty could have been reduced with additional information about key risk factors. For example, sexual orientation is one of the best predictors of sexual assault risk in civilian samples (e.g., Black et al., 2011), but it could not be included in the current analyses.[2] However, in the 2016 Workplace and Gender Relations Survey of Active Duty Members, sexual orientation and transgender status were assessed. Specifically, the survey found that men who identified themselves as gay, bisexual, or transgender made up 3 percent of all active-duty men but were exposed to more than ten times the risk of sexual assault compared with men who identified themselves as not gay, bisexual, or transgender (3.5 percent risk compared with 0.3 percent risk) (Davis, Vega, and McLeod, 2017). This finding implies that more than one-quarter of all military men who were sexually assaulted in the past year were gay, bisexual, or transgender. Furthermore, according to the survey, women who identified themselves as lesbian, bisexual, or transgender made up 12 percent of all active-duty women and faced almost twice the risk of sexual assault compared with other service women (6.3 percent risk compared with 3.5 percent risk). This implies that approximately one in five military women who were sexually assaulted in the past year were lesbian, bisexual, or transgender. Thus, it is likely that prediction of sexual assault in the military could be substantially improved by including sexual orientation in the models.

Recommendations

Our analyses suggest that several factors are associated with increased risk of sexual assault and sexual harassment among service women and men. DoD can use this infor-

---

[2] Although RAND researchers proposed to assess sexual orientation on the 2014 RMWS, related questions and measures were removed because they were judged to violate DoD personnel policy at the time.

mation to modify programs and training that address sexual assault and sexual harassment. Specifically, our results suggest the following recommendations for DoD:

- Use risk models to inform targeted prevention and response activities.
- Through outreach and victim assistance, support the needs of service members who were sexually assaulted prior to joining the military.
- Conduct research to understand the association between pre-service and recent sexual assault.
- Investigate why risk varies by service branch, occupation group, AFQT score, and other characteristics.

Furthermore, this report demonstrates that risk of sexual assault and sexual harassment can be predicted sufficiently well to produce sharply different predicted rates of victimization, especially for women and men whose predicted risk is especially low or high. This differentiation is achieved using just characteristics of the service member, his or her job, and his or her work environment. Future models of risk could substantially improve upon those described here with the addition of known risk factors that were unavailable at the time this study was conducted (such as whether the member belongs to a sexual or gender minority) and with the inclusion of more-detailed information about service members' living and work environments (such as leadership climate and workplace hostility).

Acknowledgments

We are grateful for the critical reviews and suggestions for improving this report that we received from Amy Street, of Boston University and the Women's Health Sciences Division of the U.S. Department of Veterans Affairs' National Center for PTSD, and from Susan Paddock, of the RAND Corporation.

Abbreviations

AFQT	Armed Forces Qualification Test
AIC	Akaike Information Criterion
CI	confidence interval
CONUS	continental United States
DMDC	Defense Manpower Data Center
DoD	U.S. Department of Defense
OCONUS	outside the continental United States
RMWS	RAND Military Workplace Study
ROTC	Reserve Officers' Training Corps
Tjur's D	Tjur's coefficient of discrimination
WGRA	Workplace and Gender Relations Survey of Active Duty Members

CHAPTER ONE

Introduction

In the spring of 2014, the Sexual Assault Prevention and Response Office in the Office of the Secretary of Defense asked the RAND Corporation to conduct the 2014 Workplace and Gender Relations Survey of Active Duty Members (WGRA), a congressionally required biennial survey of the state of gender relations. In consultation with experts at RAND and other institutions, a scientific advisory board, the Defense Manpower Data Center (DMDC), and Sexual Assault Prevention and Response program officials from each service, RAND researchers redesigned the survey questions used to assess each of the principal outcomes, developed a new approach to sample weighting designed to reduce nonresponse bias, and conducted a follow-up study of survey nonrespondents to examine whether their exposure to sexual assault and sexual harassment differed systematically from the weighted sample of respondents.[1] The redesigned survey, known as the RAND Military Workplace Study (RMWS), was intended to more reliably measure (1) criminal sexual assault experiences as defined in the Uniform Code of Military Justice and (2) the military equal employment violations of sexual harassment and gender discrimination as defined in DoD Directive 1350.2.

DoD, in consultation with White House national security staff, stipulated that the sample for the new study include a census of all active-duty women and 25 percent of active-duty men in the Army, Navy, Air Force, and Marine Corps. A total of 477,513 DoD active-duty service members were randomly selected from a population of 1,317,561 active-duty members who met the study inclusion criteria requiring that they be age 18 or older, below the rank of a general or flag officer, and in service for at least six months. These are the same inclusion criteria used in prior WGRAs.

The web-based survey was fielded in the summer of 2014. Of the 477,513 DoD active-duty members invited to take the survey, 145,300 individuals participated, or just more than 30 percent. The respondents included 34 percent of the women sampled (67,187) and 27.9 percent of the men (78,113). Service members in the Air Force

---

[1] The U.S. Department of Defense (DoD) requires that the following statement be included in this report: Reference to sexual assault is based on survey respondents' answers to questions about their experiences but does not reflect whether a sexual assault was substantiated by an investigation. Use of the terms *perpetrator* and *victim* in this report are not intended to presume the guilt or innocence of an individual.

had the highest response rate (43.5 percent), followed by those in the Army (29.4 percent), Navy (23.3 percent), and Marine Corps (20.6 percent).

A series of reports have been released to describe the survey design and methods (Morral, Gore, and Schell, 2014); top-line and in-depth estimates of sexual assault, sexual harassment, and gender discrimination (Morral, Gore, and Schell, 2015a, 2015b; Morral et al., 2018; National Defense Research Institute, 2014); and investigations of potential bias (Morral, Gore, and Schell, 2016). Although these reports include descriptions of the characteristics of victims, perpetrators, and assaults or incidents of harassment and discrimination, they do not include comprehensive analyses of the risk factors associated with sexual assault and sexual harassment. This report fills that analytic gap and provides leaders and policymakers with an analysis of risk factors that can be used to better inform prevention and response efforts.

In this report, we use the survey data and linked personnel records to examine the role of a wide range of demographic characteristics, service experience, and organizational characteristics in explaining individuals' risk of exposure to a sexual assault or sexual harassment in the past 12 months. The goal for these analyses is not to produce a single, multivariate model that best predicts individual risk; instead, we aim to produce interpretable estimates for the importance of each potential factor in explaining risk of sexual assault and harassment.

Producing these estimates can be a challenge because some of the factors of interest are known to influence other factors. For example, the effect of age on sexual assault risk may occur, in part, via the known and strong causal effect of age on military rank. Thus, one would not want to control for rank if trying to estimate the overall importance of age in determining risk of sexual assault. Such a model would underestimate the importance of age because part of the total effect of age is mediated through another factor in the model.[2] On the other hand, when trying to assess the importance of rank, one should control for age. This is because age could create a spurious bivariate association between sexual assault and rank by having causal effects on both factors. For our purposes, it would be inappropriate to throw all of the factors into a "kitchen sink" model. In such a model, effects for some factors would represent only the direct component of the effect, conditioned on specific mediators, while effects for other factors may be the total effect of the factor. This makes it difficult to interpret any comparisons of effect sizes across factors.

To avoid these interpretational problems, we used an approach sometimes referred to as *sequential multiple regression* (e.g., Cohen et al., 2002; Tabachnick and

---

[2] When attempting to investigate a specific theory about direct versus mediated causal effects, it is often necessary to control for hypothesized mediators while estimating the effect of a given variable (Baron and Kenny, 1986). In the present study, however, we are not attempting to investigate such a theory; rather, we seek to identify the variables that may be more important in determining risk of sexual assault. In such a case, one should avoid controlling for any variable that is plausibly an effect of the variable of interest when assessing the effect size (Cohen et al., 2002).

Fidell, 2007). In this approach, variables that are thought to temporally or causally precede other variables are entered in a sequence of models earlier than variables that are possibly influenced by the early variables. In this study, we sorted the candidate predictors (i.e., the risk factors) into four ordered classes (*tiers*) corresponding to their temporal or conceptual priority: (1) birth demographics, (2) characteristics at the time of service entry, (3) personal and career history characteristics, and (4) recent experiences. For factors in each tier, we estimated their effects while controlling for the factors in earlier tiers. Thus, we estimated the importance of the factors assuming that factors in later tiers might be influenced by factors in earlier tiers and that factors in earlier tiers were unlikely to be affected by those in later tiers.

Our general analytic approach, therefore, was to predict the prevalence of sexual assault and sexual harassment from a series of multivariate regression models that sequentially add later tiers of risk factors. We assess the effect sizes for a given factor from a model that controls for possible confounds for that factor's effect (factors from earlier tiers) but does not control for other risk factors that may be influenced by that factor (factors from later tiers).

By examining how much each factor predicts risk over and above what can be explained by conceptually prior factors, the analysis provides a more interpretable picture of the role of each factor. This information could be helpful in efforts to better target prevention interventions. Factors that are correlated with risk but explain very little of it after controlling for conceptually prior factors are likely to be poor targets for risk-reduction interventions. Conversely, factors that predict risk even after controlling for conceptually prior factors may deserve special consideration in prevention and training efforts.

This report is organized as follows: Chapter Two reviews prior research on the factors associated with sexual assault and sexual harassment in military and civilian populations. In Chapter Three, we describe our data sources, statistical models, and methods of describing effect sizes. Chapters Four and Five present modeling results for sexual assault risk and sexual harassment risk, respectively. In Chapter Six, we discuss the significance of the results, how they correspond to prior work in this area, and what we think the U.S. military should do in response to our findings. Finally, the appendix provides algorithms for calculating sexual assault risk for women and men using a simplified model of risk that uses only risk factors that are easily available in DMDC data.

CHAPTER TWO

Previous Research on Risk Factors for Sexual Assault and Sexual Harassment

Prior research has considered various risk factors for sexual assault and sexual harassment. Although much of this work has been conducted using civilian samples, there is a growing body of research to confirm risk factors shared across civilian and military groups and to identify risk factors unique to the military. In this chapter, we summarize this existing research.

Risk of Sexual Assault

Some advocates and researchers have argued that sexual assault is an event controlled by the perpetrator and that, as a result, investigation of victim characteristics is misplaced. Moreover, such research may promote victim-blaming. Because of these views, empirical research on victim characteristics was limited until relatively recently. Over the past 20 years or so, researchers have shifted toward examining victim characteristics as a strategy to identify high-risk groups and ultimately design and deliver effective prevention programs (e.g., Adams-Curtis and Forbes, 2004).

Sexual Assault Risk Associated with Target Demographic Characteristics

Several demographic characteristics are associated with sexual assault victimization; these include gender, age, marital status, sexual orientation, race, and educational attainment. According to results from a large, nationally representative survey, women are 11 times more likely than men to be raped during their lifetime (Breiding et al., 2014; see also Michael et al., 1994; Tjaden and Thoennes, 1998). The discrepant risk carried by women is also true in the military. In 2014, 4.9 percent of active-duty service women experienced a sexual assault in the previous year, whereas 0.9 percent of active-duty service men had been assaulted (Jaycox et al., 2015; see also Kessler, 2014). In both civilian and military populations, younger adults bear significantly greater risk of sexual assault than older adults do (Kilpatrick et al., 1997; Kimerling et al., 2007; LeardMann et al., 2013; Street, Rosellini, et al., 2016; Street, Stafford, et al., 2008). Regardless of age, women and men who are single or divorced are at increased risk of sexual assault relative to married people (Kimerling et al., 2007; LeardMann et al., 2013; Street, Rosellini, et al., 2016; see also Sadler et al., 2003; Street, Stafford, et al., 2008). This may be partly because younger and single adults are more likely to date or attend social gatherings, where they have increased exposure to potential perpetrators (Marx, Wie, and Gross, 1996), or because such people are targeted by perpetrators. Using administrative databases of all U.S. Army soldiers, Street and colleagues reported that the odds of administratively reporting a sexual assault were 1.3 times higher for unmarried soldiers than for married soldiers (Street, Rosellini, et al., 2016). Relative to heterosexual individuals, lesbian, gay, and bisexual men and women appear to be at elevated risk of lifetime sexual assault: Across 75 studies that assessed the prevalence of sexual assault against sexual minorities, the median estimate of lifetime sexual assault against gay and bisexual men was 30 percent, and the median estimate of lifetime sexual assault against lesbian and bisexual women was 43 percent (Rothman, Exner, and Baughman, 2011).

There are inconsistent findings regarding the relationship between race and sexual assault risk. Some research using large and nationally representative samples has shown similar lifetime prevalence of rape among black (21.2 percent; 95% confidence interval [CI]: 17.2–25.9) and white women (20.5 percent; 95% CI: 18.8–22.3) (Breiding et al., 2014), but other similar research shows higher lifetime rates of rape among black women (23.4 percent) than among white women (15.4 percent) (Kilpatrick et al., 2007). For research focused on service members, one study found that a smaller proportion of non-Hispanic white service members (1.5 percent) indicated that they had experienced unwanted sexual contact in the previous year relative to minority-group service members (2.5 percent) (DMDC, 2013a), but an Army study found that being non-Hispanic white was associated with increased risk of sexual victimization among soldiers (Kessler, 2014). The odds of administratively reporting a sexual assault are higher among non-Hispanic white Army women than among women of other races (Street, Rosellini, et al., 2016), which suggests that white service women may be more likely than minorities to report an assault when it does occur. In contrast, data from the Millennium Cohort Study, a DoD study of 150,000 service members enrolled between 2001 and 2008, showed no relationship between race and a single survey item assessing sexual assault during military service (LeardMann et al., 2013). In studies focusing on veterans, data have been inconsistent. A report on veterans seeking care from the Veterans Health Administration found that white veterans—both men and women—were more likely than minorities to screen positive for military sexual trauma (Kimerling et al., 2007). However, in a national survey of veterans, race was unrelated to sexual assault victimization during military service (Sadler et al., 2003).

The relationship between educational attainment and sexual assault is also unclear. In a prospective study of a nationally representative sample of civilian women, educational attainment was not significantly associated with sexual assault (Kilpatrick et al., 1997). Lower levels of education have predicted sexual assault in the military (Kessler, 2014; LeardMann et al., 2013; Sadler et al., 2003; Street, Rosellini, et al., 2016), but *higher* levels of education predicted a combined sexual harassment and sexual assault measure among reservists (Street, Stafford, et al., 2008). In a sample of female veterans who served from the Vietnam War to Gulf War era, women who had completed college (18.3 percent) were less likely than women who had not (33.9 percent) to indicate that they had been raped during their military service (Sadler et al., 2003).

In one study, the Armed Forces Qualification Test (AFQT) score (a measure of general aptitude) was not one of the top 20 predictors of sexual assault victimization among soldiers, but there was a significant inverse association: Higher AFQT scores predicted lower sexual assault victimization risk (Kessler, 2014). Similarly, higher AFQT scores predicted lower risk of sexual assault perpetration.

Many of the demographic risk factors reviewed in this section correspond with lower sociocultural power. In a study of sexual assault in the military workplace, Harned and colleagues (2002) combined age (younger), marital status (unmarried), race (minority racial group), and level of education (lower) into a general indicator of respondents' limited sociocultural power. Relying on a large sample of service members, the authors found that lower sociocultural power was associated with experiencing unwanted sexual contact in the military (Harned et al., 2002).

Risk Associated with Past Sexual Assault

For both women and men, experiencing a sexual assault in the past is strongly associated with recent sexual assault victimization (Classen, Palesh, and Aggarwal, 2005; Coxell et al., 1999; Elliott, Mok, and Briere, 2004; Gidycz et al., 1993; Humphrey and White, 2000; Lalor and McElvaney, 2010; Littleton, Axsom, and Grills-Taquechel, 2009; Messman-Moore, Brown, and Koelsch, 2005; Roodman and Clum, 2001). This relationship holds in military populations as well. For example, among female Navy recruits, women who were sexually victimized as children were 4.8 times more likely than nonvictimized women to indicate that they had unwanted sexual experiences consistent with rape during their military service (Merrill et al., 1999). Using an Army sample, Kessler (2014) replicated this finding, showing that women who had been sexually assaulted prior to enlistment experienced more sexual workplace violence. Similarly, the Millennium Cohort Study showed that service women who reported prior sexual stressors were three times more likely to indicate that they were sexual assaulted during the prospective, three-year follow-up (LeardMann et al., 2013).[1] Veteran samples have also replicated this general finding (Sadler et al., 2003).

The mechanisms that create the association between prior sexual assault and recent sexual assault are not well understood. Any risk factor for sexual assault that is stable over time could give rise to this correlation. Stable victim characteristics, such as the victim's personality, relationship style, mental health, or sexual orientation, may be

---

[1] *Sexual stressors* were defined as having "suffered forced sexual relations or sexual assault" or "experienced sexual harassment" (LeardMann et al., 2013, p. e216).

characteristics that attract perpetrators at any point in time, elevating the victim's risk of assault throughout their lives. Stable situational factors, such as continued proximity to a prior perpetrator (perhaps a spouse or other family member) or living in a location with a high rate of sexual assault, are a second possible class of mechanisms that could create this association. Another hypothesized class of mechanisms are changes that occur to the victim because of the earlier assault that then increase the risk of future assaults. For example, prior coercive sexual relationships may make such behavior appear normal, inhibiting the victim's ability to detect and avoid it. Alternatively, the earlier sexual assault may result in the victim finding a much wider range of sexual contact to be unwanted, increasing the risk of experiencing unwanted sexual contact.

Finally, it is possible that a portion of the strong association of prior sexual assault with recent sexual assault can be attributed to some type of measurement error. For example, reporting a specific sexual assault on a survey or experiencing a recent sexual assault may cue respondents' memory of similar incidents in their past, making it more likely that they report those incidents on the survey (regardless of whether they were actually more likely to have those experiences). It is also possible that recent sexual assault experiences could cause the victim to reinterpret earlier ambiguous or unpleasant sexual experiences in a way that results in them being counted as sexual assault. Alternatively, it is possible that some respondents have response biases to questions about sexual assault and may be unwilling to admit to such experiences even if they occurred. Such biases would inflate the number of individuals who appear to have never been sexually assaulted, which, in turn, would cause studies to overestimate the association between prior and recent sexual assaults.

Many studies (e.g., Messman-Moore and Long, 2000) have investigated specific factors that might contribute to this association; however, none of the studies is able to identify the relative importance of the many hypothesized mechanisms that could create an association between prior and recent sexual assault. For example, several studies have shown that women with victimization experiences use alcohol more often and more heavily than other women (Abbey et al., 1996; Champion et al., 2004; Larimer et al., 1999; McMullin and White, 2006; Mohler-Kuo et al., 2004) and are more likely to be in situations where they are exposed to potential perpetrators who are drinking (Single and Wortley, 1993; Testa and Livingston, 2009; Vogler, 1994). Other research has shown that sexual assault victims are slower than nonvictims to identify coercive or manipulative sexual interactions as problematic (Wilson, Calhoun, and Bernat, 1999). Similarly, other researchers have documented differences in personality or relationship styles between victims and nonvictims (Norris, Nurius, and Dimeff, 1996; Schry and White, 2013). However, this body of research does not yet support any strong conclusions about which mechanisms are most important for producing the association between prior and recent sexual assault within civilian samples, and it is difficult to know the extent to which the factors that have been studied generalize to military samples.

Risk Associated with Military Characteristics

Several military characteristics predict sexual assault risk. Most consistently across studies, there is clear evidence that enlisted service members—particularly those at lower ranks—carry a greater risk than do officers (LeardMann et al., 2013; Jaycox et al., 2015; Sadler et al., 2003; Street, Rosellini, et al., 2016). There is also converging evidence that members of the Air Force are at lower risk than members of other branches are (LeardMann et al., 2013). Prior analyses on the data being using for the current analysis have already shown such differences, as well as that these differences persist while controlling for the demographic factors and military characteristics that differentiate service branches (Schell and Morral, 2015a).

Other military characteristics have been included more sporadically in studies of service members; therefore, replicability is less certain. For example, in a study of a large cohort of service women, LeardMann and colleagues (2013) reported that combat specialists were at increased risk of sexual assault victimization, whereas health care specialists and functional support personnel were at lower risk. This study also found that women who had completed a combat deployment in the previous three years were at increased risk of combined sexual harassment and sexual assault (but not sexual assault alone) (LeardMann et al., 2013). In a study of Army members, basic training and transitioning between duty stations were identified as periods of increased risk of sexual assault among both women and men (Street, Rosellini, et al., 2016).

When developing a model of sexual assault in the military workplace, Harned and colleagues (2002) conceived the combination of pay grade (ranging from E1 to O6 continuously) and years of active service as a measure of military organization power; the study confirmed that the construct was negatively associated with sexual assault.

Finally, military settings in which a work group is disproportionately male confer greater risk than settings with lower percentages of male service members (Harned et al., 2002; Sadler et al., 2003). Most perpetrators of sexual assaults against service members are men (Jaycox et al., 2015), so this effect may be simply explained by noting that as the proportion of potential offenders in an environment increases, so does an individual's risk of sexual assault. Other studies have focused on cultural factors and found that workplaces that are disproportionately male may also be marked by hyper-masculinity, sexual harassment, and male dominance in the power hierarchy (Turchik and Wilson, 2010). Indeed, Harned and colleagues (2002) found that the relationship between disproportionately male work environments and increased risk of sexual assault was completely mediated by the increase in sexual harassment in these environments.

Risk of Sexual Harassment and Gender Discrimination

Understanding the demographic and military characteristics of service members who have the highest risk of being sexually harassed or discriminated against may help leaders and policymakers better monitor work environments and institute changes that protect the most vulnerable. In this section, we provide a high-level review of risk factors associated with sexual harassment and gender discrimination in the military.

Risk Associated with Victim Demographic Characteristics

Risk of sexual harassment is associated with gender, age, marital status, educational attainment, and race. Across studies of working adults, women are consistently more likely than men to be sexually harassed (Martindale, 1991; McDonald, 2012; Stockdale, Visio, and Batra, 1999; U.S. Merit Systems Protection Board, 1995). In 2014, active-duty service women were 3.5 times more likely than active-duty service men to indicate having experiences consistent with sexual harassment or gender discrimination (Farris et al., 2015). Among current and former reservists, the same pattern holds: Relative to male reservists, female reservists have a higher risk of sexual harassment (Schell and Morral, 2015b; Street, Gradus, et al., 2007).

Harned and colleagues (2002) examined multiple characteristics that correspond to service women's power in the organization. A composite of age (younger), level of education (lower), race (minority), and marital status (nonmarried) was used to signify lower sociocultural power and was associated with increased risk of sexual harassment in the military (Harned et al., 2002). When examined separately, younger age, lower educational attainment, and nonmarried status have been reported by other researchers to predict sexual harassment (LeardMann et al., 2013; McDonald, 2012).

However, the association between race and risk of sexual harassment is complex. In civilian samples, white women are less likely than other women to experience sexual harassment (Berdahl and Moore, 2006; Bergman and Drasgow, 2003; Kalof et al., 2001). However, in some military samples, this association did not hold (LeardMann et al., 2013), or it appeared in the opposite direction, with white women experiencing more sexual harassment than other women (Buchanan, Settles, and Woods, 2008). When the specific types of sexual harassment were disaggregated, Buchanan, Settles, and Woods (2008) reported that white service women were more likely than black service women to indicate experiencing crude behavior (e.g., repeated, offensive sexual jokes) and gender discrimination. However, black service women were more likely than white service women to indicate that they had experienced unwanted sexual attention (e.g., unwanted attempts to stroke, fondle, or kiss) and *quid pro quo* harassment (Buchanan, Settles, and Woods, 2008). Based on data from the 2012 WGRA, white service members (men and women combined) were less likely to have experiences consistent with sexual harassment (6 percent) than minority service members were (8 percent) (DMDC, 2013b).

Risk Associated with Military Characteristics

Fitzgerald and colleagues (1997) proposed an explanatory model of sexual harassment that posited two major antecedents (or risk factors) for sexual harassment. The first antecedent—job gender context, which described the extent to which the work was masculinized—was measured as the percentage of the workforce that was male, whether the individual's supervisor was male, and the extent to which women were rare in the work environment. The second antecedent—organizational context—was measured as either the individual's or the shared workforce's perception regarding the risk associated with reporting sexual harassment, the extent to which allegations were taken seriously, and the likelihood of meaningful sanctions. The model was originally validated with a sample of women working a large utility company and showed that women working in settings that were masculinized or that tolerated sexual harassment were more likely to experience sexual harassment (Fitzgerald et al., 1997).

Since then, these same risk factors have been examined and replicated in military samples. Using data from the 1995 WGRA, Fitzgerald, Drasgow, and Magley (1999) found that sexual harassment of both men and women was less likely when respondents worked in settings where the gender ratio was less skewed toward men and when the respondents perceived positive leadership efforts to stop sexual harassment (see also Harned et al., 2002; Willness, Steel, and Lee, 2007).

In a similar model that included organization and gender context, Harned and colleagues (2002) examined individual characteristics that correspond to organizational power within the military. A composite of pay grade (varied continuously from E1 to O6) and years of active service was used to assess the construct. Consistent with the researchers' prediction, organizational power was negatively associated with sexual harassment risk (Harned et al., 2002). When examined separately, studies show that enlisted service members are at higher risk for sexual harassment than officers are (Buchanan, Settles, and Woods, 2008; LeardMann et al., 2013). Within these groups, junior enlisted service members (E1–E4) are at higher risk than senior enlisted service members (E5–E9), and junior officers (O1–O3) are at higher risk than senior officers (O4–O6) (Farris et al., 2015).

Perhaps the most elemental military characteristic is service branch (Army, Navy, Air Force, Marine Corps). Across iterations of the WGRA, Air Force members had the lowest rate of sexual harassment among the service branches (DMDC, 2011; DMDC, 2013a; see also LeardMann et al., 2013). Prior analysis of the current data set (the 2014 RMWS survey) found that, even while controlling for demographic and military differences across the services (age, educational attainment, deployment, gender ratio), women in the Marine Corps, Army, and Navy are 1.6–1.9 times more likely than women in the Air Force to experience sexual harassment (Schell and Morral, 2015a). Similarly, men in the Marine Corps, Army, and Navy are 1.3–2.3 times more likely than men in the Air Force to experience sexual harassment (Schell and Morral, 2015a). This analysis ruled out several demographic and military characteristics that could have, but did not, explain the lower risk experienced by airmen. More research is necessary to identify the source of the differences; possibilities include "culture, training, policy, or programmatic differences between the Air Force and other services" (Schell and Morral, 2015a, p. 68).

When examining the deployment experiences of a large sample of military service members, LeardMann and colleagues (2013) reported that service women with combat deployments had the highest incidence of sexual harassment. Service women who deployed and had combat-like experiences on deployment were 2.2 times more likely than other women to indicate that they had been sexually harassed. In addition, among service women, combat specialists had a greater risk of sexual harassment than health care specialists did (LeardMann et al., 2013).

Summary

Published research suggests that women, both civilians and those in the military, are more likely than men to be sexually assaulted or sexually harassed. In addition, younger adults and those who are single or divorced appear to be at higher risk of sexual assault and sexual harassment than older adults and those who are married, respectively. Results addressing the extent to which race is associated with sexual assault risk are inconsistent, and the association between race and sexual harassment among those in the military is complex. Lower academic performance appears to be associated with sexual assault victimization, and lower educational attainment is associated with increased risk of sexual harassment.

When we focus on military characteristics, prior research shows that service members in the Air Force appear to be at lower risk of sexual assault and sexual harassment than those in other services are. Overall, enlisted service members are at higher risk of sexual assault and sexual harassment than officers are. Within these groups, junior enlisted and junior officers have a higher risk of sexual assault and harassment than do more-senior enlisted and senior officers, respectively. Initial research suggests that disproportionately male military work groups might be associated with greater risk of sexual assault and sexual harassment. In addition, research has suggested that women who combat deploy are at increased risk of combined sexual assault and sexual harassment. Risk of sexual assault and sexual harassment may differ by occupation in the military; for instance, combat specialists appear to face higher risks than health care specialists do.

Finally, research suggests a strong association between recent sexual assault experiences and earlier sexual assaults experiences. However, this association is difficult to interpret because the literature does not currently support conclusions about which of many possible mechanisms give rise to it.

CHAPTER THREE

Approach to Estimating Effect Sizes

To investigate risk factors for sexual assault and sexual harassment in the military, we clustered risk factors into groups and then put them in temporal or logical order, from those that are more elemental and stable (e.g., birth demographics, such as race and gender) to those that describe a service member's environment in the past year (e.g., installation characteristics, such as average age and gender ratio). Our general approach to exploring risk factors for sexual assault and sexual harassment in the military was to use regression models to estimate the association between each identified factor and the risk of sexual assault and harassment.

In this report, we provide the following three associations between risk and each factor:

1. the *bivariate* association between each factor and sexual assault or sexual harassment risk
2. *adjusted for prior tiers* associations, which are estimated while controlling for all factors that were specified as conceptually or logically prior to the factor of interest
3. *adjusted, including current tier* associations, which control for (1) the factors that were conceptually prior to the factor of interest and (2) other risk factors in the same tier that were neither conceptually prior nor conceptually subsequent to the factor of interest.

The third type of association is included for readers who would like to see estimated effects using a larger set of covariates. The specific additional covariates are discussed in the text.

This chapter provides details about the data and analytic approach used to construct these estimates.

RAND Military Workplace Study and Data

Data used for our analyses include administrative data provided by DMDC and survey data collected as part of the RMWS. In early 2014, DoD asked the RAND National

Defense Research Institute to conduct an independent assessment of sexual assault, sexual harassment, and gender discrimination in the military. The RMWS survey was one of the largest surveys of its kind: A representative sample of almost 560,000 active-duty and reserve-component service members were invited to participate, and more than 170,000 completed the web-administered survey. Although the RMWS includes a small number of respondents from the reserve component and the Coast Guard, the present analyses focus exclusively on results from active-component members of the four DoD services.

Details of the overall study design can be found in Volume 1 of this report series (Morral, Gore, and Schell, 2014). The RMWS sampled 100 percent of active-component women and 25 percent of active-component men in the DoD services. Within gender groups, personnel were sampled with equal probability. Most respondents received the new survey instrument developed by RAND. A random sample instead received an older version of the WGRA so that we could compare rates of sexual harassment and unwanted sexual contact across the two forms. While all respondents randomized to the new RAND instrument received the sexual assault module, approximately 44 percent of respondents who received the RAND form were skipped out of the full harassment module to reduce survey response burden. Thus, for the sexual assault risk models described in this report, we used information on past-year sexual assault from 115,759 active-duty service members (62,161 men and 53,598 women), and for the sexual harassment risk models, we used information on past-year sexual harassment from 65,539 service members (35,443 men and 30,096 women).

Statistical Methods

Effect Size Metrics

Our choice of statistical methods was driven by a desire to provide useful estimates of the effect sizes of a wide range of potential risk factors. To do this, we used two different methods of computing the effect size of each factor predicting sexual assault: a risk ratio and a Tjur's coefficient of discrimination (Tjur's D). The risk ratio assesses the prevalence of sexual assault for individuals with a particular value on a risk factor relative to those with some other value. When looking at gender, for example, if 5 percent of women experienced sexual assault and 1 percent of men experienced sexual assault, the bivariate risk ratio for women relative to men is 5/1 = 5; that is, women have five times the risk of sexual assault as men do. Similarly, if we measure age in decades, a risk ratio of 0.5 implies that risk of sexual assault is cut in half for each additional decade in age, while a risk ratio of 1 indicates no effect of the variable.

Risk ratios are a common and useful way to describe the strength of associations when comparing sexual assault risk across individual service members. However, this effect size metric does not assess how well the risk factor can account for sexual assault risk across the entire military. A variable may have a very large risk ratio, but if that high risk applies to a very small portion of the military, the variable will not explain many of the sexual assaults in the military. To assess the importance of the various risk factors across the full military, we used Tjur's D, also called Tjur's R^2 (Tjur, 2009). This is a pseudo-R^2 for use with dichotomous outcomes. It has a straightforward interpretation as the difference between (1) the mean predicted probability for those who experienced the outcome and (2) the mean predicted probability for those who did not experience the outcome. That is, the Tjur's D indicates how effectively the entire regression model differentiates the risks of those who were sexually assaulted from those who were not. Although referred to as a pseudo-R^2 measure, it is not directly comparable in magnitude to the more common R^2 from a linear model, and its numeric value is generally smaller than is found with linear models.[1] It also tends to be smallest for models predicting rate outcomes, so it is most useful for understanding which factors or groups of factors contribute most to the prediction of a particular outcome. We converted these Tjur's D values to percentages, where a value of 100 percent indicates that the model perfectly predicts every single sexual assault in the military, and a value of 0 percent indicates that the model provides no information about which individuals are at increased or decreased risk.

The Tjur's D is computed for any given model, not for individual factors within that model. When looking at individual factors within a model that includes covariates, we estimated the change in Tjur's D (Δ Tjur's D), which indicates how much the value improves in a model that includes a particular risk factor relative to the value in a model that omits only that factor. It is worth noting that this model performance indicator is not precisely identical to the loss function used in the estimation of the regression model, so it is possible that the value declines slightly when adding another factor, if that factor was a weak predictor (Tjur, 2009).

Statistical Models

Our general analytic approach was to predict the prevalence of sexual assault and sexual harassment from a series of increasingly complex regression models, beginning with bivariate models (one risk factor at a time) and moving to more-complex models that include appropriate sets of covariates for understanding the effect of a given factor. When estimating Tjur's D effect sizes, we used standard logistic regression models (i.e., logit link function). When estimating risk ratios, we used Poisson regression models (i.e., logarithmic link function) with robust standard errors (Chu and Cole, 2010; Zou, 2004). These models were chosen over the typical logistic regression models because they directly return risk ratios and their confidence intervals rather than odds ratios,

---

[1] More generally, it is somewhat misleading to think of any pseudo-R^2 measure used with dichotomous outcomes as *variance accounted for* by the entire model. For logistic regression, the error of prediction varies as a function of the specific model-predicted probabilities and is not a constant for the model (Cohen et al., 2002). Rather, the error of prediction varies for each case based on its specific predictor values.

which are more difficult to interpret. All models were estimated with survey weights to account for survey design and nonresponse using the survey package in the R statistical program. (For a detailed description of the sample weights, see Ghosh-Dastidar, Schell, and Morral, 2014.)

All regression models were run separately for women and men. As a result, the models allow for any interactions between the various risk factors and gender and always control for gender.

Sequence of Regression Models

As discussed earlier, estimates of effect sizes can be used for a range of purposes. When these effect sizes are used to describe the groups of service members who are at high risk of sexual assault (or sexual harassment), it is often most useful to estimate bivariate effects, such as bivariate risk ratios. Bivariate effect sizes quantify how much information about sexual assault risk each individual factor can provide. However, bivariate effect sizes are often misleading if they are used to try to understand why some individuals are at high risk of sexual assault or which risk factors are important. For example, if one is trying to determine who to target with additional sexual assault prevention training, it is useful to know that service members with an E4 pay grade have 1.5 times greater sexual assault risk than those with an E5 pay grade. However, it may be an error to conclude that promoting someone from E4 to E5 (without changing any of his or her other factors) would suddenly reduce that persons' risk of sexual assault.

When using the modeling results to better understand why some individuals are at higher or lower risk of sexual assault, one almost always wants to estimate covariate-adjusted effect sizes, such as adjusted risk ratios. For each risk factor, it is best to control for any other factors that could create a causally spurious association between that factor and sexual assault risk—that is, any factor that could be the cause of both that factor and sexual assault. For example, E5 members are, on average, about four years older than E4 members, and we know that age is one of the factors that determines pay grade. Thus, age may be an alternative explanation of any bivariate effect of pay grade on sexual assault. To understand the extent to which changes in pay grade may change sexual assault risk, one should estimate adjusted risk ratios that control for logically antecedent risk factors, such as age and gender, that cannot be altered by changes in pay grade but that can have an indirect effect on risk through pay grade (Cohen et al., 2002).

For each risk factor we examined for this study, we identified the other risk factors that were temporally or logically antecedent to that risk factor. We then controlled for those antecedent factors when producing adjusted effect size estimates (both adjusted risk ratios and change in Tjur's D). Thus, the adjusted effect sizes controlled for a set of covariates that was tailored to each risk factor. When investigating the effect of pay grade, for example, we controlled for risk factors determined at the time of birth (gender, age, race), as well as risk factors that were known at the time each member entered service (e.g., service branch, AFQT score). The selection of covariates was done by grouping the risk factors into four tiers:

1. birth demographics
2. characteristics at the time of service entry
3. personal and career history (factors that may change after entry into service)
4. recent experiences (factors that were known only in the past year).

When producing adjusted risk estimates, the effect for any given factor was estimated using a regression model that controlled for all the factors in the earlier tiers. In addition, all effect sizes controlled for gender because models were stratified by gender.

Table 3.1 lists the four tiers and the risk factors that constitute each tier. The table thus indicates each set of factors used when producing the adjusted effect size estimates. The list includes many of the risk factors identified in previous research as possibly associated with sexual assault or sexual harassment risk. These factors include age, race, AFQT score, pre-service sexual assault, pay grade, service branch, occupation group, educational attainment, marital status, number of dependents, deployment history, percentage of the workforce that is male, and recent separation from the military. As a result of conversations with sexual assault prevention officials at DoD and the availability of relevant data, we added the following to these previously studied factors: entry type, service location inside the continental United States (CONUS) or outside the continental United States (OCONUS), and assignment to a ship. We also added characteristics of the service members' recent work environment, including their duty unit; the postal code of the service member's duty unit, which is a proxy for the installation where the member was assigned; and the major command in which the member served, as described by the major command code (for the Army, Navy, and Air Force) or monitored command code (for the Marine Corps). Some of the specific risk factors in these subgroups include the percentage of leadership positions held by men; the number of personnel in the unit, installation, or command; and the average age in each environment. All risk factors were derived from administrative data sets provided by DMDC—chiefly, the Active Duty Military Personnel Master File and the Defense Enrollment Eligibility Reporting System database—except for pre-service sexual assault, which was derived from a RMWS survey item asking about exposure to experiences that would qualify as a sexual assault before joining the military (question SAFU40; see Morral, Gore, and Schell, 2014, Appendix A).

The determination of which risk factors are conceptually prior—and therefore should be controlled for when producing adjusted effect sizes—is partially subjective. Because of this, we grouped predictor factors into a highly approximate causal ordering, and we do not assess how effect sizes for individual factors might change after controlling for all combinations of other factors within the same tier as the predictor factor. For example, the adjusted risk ratio for the association between the size of one's

Table 3.1
Risk Factors Investigated, by Tier

Tier	Subgroup	Risk Factor	Levels or Scale
Tier 1: Birth demographics	Not applicable	Age	Per decade
		Race	Asian; black; Hispanic; other; **white**
Tier 2: Characteristics at the time of service entry	Not applicable	AFQT score (enlisted only)	Per 10 percentile points
		Pre-service sexual assault	Yes; **no**
		Entry type	**Enlisted (including warrant officers and those who went through Officer Candidate School)**; officer, academy; officer, Reserve Officers' Training Corps (ROTC); officer, other
		Service branch	Army; Navy; **Air Force**; Marine Corps
Tier 3: Personal and career history	Home life	Marital status	Single; **other**
		Number of dependents	Per each dependent
		Educational attainment	**Up to high school diploma**; some college; bachelor's degree; graduate degree
	Career	Pay grade	E1–E3; **E4**; E5–E6; E7–E9; O1–O3; O4–O6; W1–W5
		Promotion speed[a]	Per year
		Past deployment (2001–2013)[b]	Per year
		Occupation group (enlisted)	Infantry, gun crews, and seamanship specialists; electronic equipment repairers; communications and intelligence specialists; health care specialists; functional support and administration; **electrical/ mechanical equipment repairers**; craftsworkers; service and supply handlers; nonoccupational
		Occupation group (officer)	**Tactical operations officers**; intelligence officers; engineering and maintenance officers; scientists and professionals; health care officers; administrators; supply, procurement, and allied officers; other

Table 3.1—Continued

Tier	Subgroup	Risk Factor	Levels or Scale
Tier 4: Recent experiences	Recent history (past 12 months)	Deployed in the past 12 months	Yes; **no**
		Location	OCONUS; **CONUS**
		Assigned to a ship[c]	Per fraction of the year
	Past-year organizational characteristics: Unit identification code	Number of personnel	Per 1,000 members
		Average age	Per year
		Percentage male	Per 10 percentage points
		Percentage male leadership[d]	Per 10 percentage points
	Past-year organizational characteristics: Postal code	Number of personnel	Per 10,000 members
		Average age	Per year
		Percentage male	Per 10 percentage points
		Percentage male leadership[d]	Per 10 percentage points
	Past-year organizational characteristics: Major or monitored command code	Number of personnel	Per 10,000 members
		Average age	Per year
		Percentage male	Per 10 percentage points
		Percentage male leadership[d]	Per 10 percentage points
	Separation from the military	Separated from military	Yes; **no**

NOTES: All models are run separately by gender, so all adjusted effect sizes control for gender. **Bold text** in the last column indicates the reference group (denominator) of categorical factors when defining relative risk ratios. To calculate risk ratios, we selected the reference group for each factor to be a category that was large and that had among the highest or lowest sexual assault risk for women. All risk factors were derived from data in the Defense Enrollment Eligibility Reporting System database, except for pre-service sexual assault, which was assessed in the RMWS.

[a] Number of years of active federal military service minus the average length of service for others in the service member's pay grade. Thus, lower numbers indicate individuals who quickly rose to their current rank.

[b] Number of years spent on deployments between September 11, 2001, and July 2013.

[c] Length of ship assignment based on months during the year with a duty unit that has a fleet post office code.

[d] Within the cluster, the percentage of leadership that is male minus the percentage of all personnel that is male.

unit and sexual assault risk does not control for the percentage of the unit that is male; both factors are in the same tier. However, some readers may want to expand the list of covariates used in producing an adjusted risk ratio to include such factors. To help accommodate this, we added a second type of adjusted effect size that includes additional covariates. Specifically, this second type of adjusted effect size includes all factors from the primary *adjusted for prior tiers* model for a given factor but adds to the model other factors that are in the same tier subgroup as that factor. For convenience, we label these estimates *adjusted, including current tier* to distinguish them from the adjusted estimates discussed earlier.

These *adjusted, including current tier* estimates provide additional controls relative to the *adjusted for prior tiers* estimates; however, the reader should be cautioned from assuming that they are generally better. Because the temporal and causal links among risk factors in the same tier are more uncertain than the links among factors in other tiers, it is possible that controlling for these factors may give less accurate estimates of the causal effect of any given risk factor. Finally, we also present Tjur's D effect size for each tier of model when added to the prior tiers. These effects quantify how much additional information about sexual assault risk is added when we add all of the factors within a tier.

Summary

To assess the relationships between risk factors and sexual assault and sexual harassment in the military, we relied on regression models to estimate bivariate effect sizes, as well as two covariate-adjusted effect sizes based on theoretically justified models. In the next chapters, we use the results of these models to describe the risk factors for sexual assault (Chapter Four) and sexual harassment (Chapter Five).

Risk Factors for Sexual Assault

In this chapter, we consider potential risk factors for sexual assault in the past year among service members. We assess risk factors first among service women and then among service men. Because the model results are separated by gender, the models do not explicitly provide effect sizes for gender as a predictor of sexual assault. However, the bivariate effect size for gender is relatively large: The risk ratio of women relative to men is 5.13 (95% CI: 4.22–6.24; Tjur's D = 1.29 percentage points).

Sexual Assault Risk Factors for Service Women

In considering the sexual assault risk factors for service women, we first assess the association between birth demographic risk factors (Tier 1) and past-year sexual assault. We then consider characteristics at the time of service entry (Tier 2), personal and career history (Tier 3), and recent experiences (Tier 4).

Birth Demographics

Table 4.1 presents bivariate and multivariate associations between past-year sexual assault of women and their age and race. Associations are expressed as risk ratios between those with a given risk factor (or with a higher value on a scale) and risk to a reference group. For instance, for the bivariate associations and those with age and race together in a single model, each additional decade in age is associated with a reduction in women's risk of sexual assault by more than 50 percent (risk ratio = 0.42; 95% CI: 0.39–0.46). Similarly, black and Asian women face significantly lower risk of sexual assault than white women. In the multivariate (*adjusted, including current tier*) model, which controls for age, Hispanic women also have significantly lower risk of sexual assault than white women.

The risk ratios in Table 4.1 document how risk of sexual assault varies across individuals with different factors, but if a factor is rare in the population, it may do little to explain the distribution of risk throughout the military. The Tjur's D values offer another measure of effect size that captures how much of risk across the military is explained by each factor. To illustrate, consider that the average rate of sexual assaults

Table 4.1
Tier 1: Association Between Birth Demographics and Past-Year Sexual Assault, Women

Risk Factor	Bivariate			Adjusted, Including Current Tier	
	Risk Ratio (95% CI)	p-value	Tjur's D	Adjusted Risk Ratio (95% CI)	p-value
Age (decades)	0.42 (0.39–0.46)	0.00	1.37	0.43 (0.39–0.47)	0.00
Race		0.00	0.17		0.00
Asian	0.54 (0.40–0.72)			0.58 (0.44–0.78)	
Black	0.71 (0.62–0.82)			0.75 (0.65–0.85)	
Hispanic	0.87 (0.73–1.04)			0.81 (0.68–0.96)	
Other	1.24 (0.98–1.57)			1.08 (0.86–1.36)	
White	1 (reference)			1 (reference)	

NOTE: We scaled Tjur's D by a factor of 100 to put it on a percentage-point scale.

against all women in the military was 4.9 percent, based on the 2014 RMWS. Therefore, if we knew nothing about women in the military who either were or were not
sexually assaulted in the past year, we would predict that both groups had a 4.9-percent
risk of having been assaulted. Thus, the Tjur's D would be zero. The bivariate association of age and sexual assault risk in Table 4.1 lists a Tjur's D of 1.37 percentage
points. This means that age can be used to differentiate risk. Specifically, the model
including age generated an average predicted probability among women who were
sexually assaulted of approximately 6.2 percent, while the average predicted probability
among women who were not sexually assaulted was 4.8 percent. That is a difference of
1.37 percentage points, which is the Tjur's D value for this factor. Tjur's D indicates
how well the prediction model differentiates the risk faced by those who were assaulted
from the risk faced by those who were not. Race, with a bivariate Tjur's D value of
0.17 percentage points, is not nearly as good at identifying who was or was not sexually
assaulted in the prior year.

The predicted risk of sexual assault for the model including only Tier 1 factors
had a Tjur's D of 1.52, with an average predicted risk of sexual assault of 4.8 percent
among service women who had no past-year assault and 6.3 percent among those who
did. (For a complete list of each tier's Tjur's D value for predicting sexual assault, for
both women and men, see Table 4.9 toward the end of this chapter.)

Characteristics at the Time of Service Entry

Table 4.2 provides three sets of associations for the service members' characteristics at entry: bivariate associations with past-year sexual assault, associations with sexual assault controlling for the Tier 1 factors (birth demographics) (the *adjusted for prior tiers* model), and multivariate model results in which birth demographics and all characteristics at the time of service entry are both included in the model (the *adjusted, including current tier* model). The most striking effect among the characteristics at entry is also possibly the most complex. Specifically, service women who reported experiences consistent with sexual assault prior to joining the military were substantially more likely to have had a sexual assault in the past year. In all three models, these women have approximately four times the risk of a past-year sexual assault compared with women reporting no pre-service sexual assault, and the magnitude of the effect, as indicated by the Tjur's D statistic, is large. As noted, the model including only birth demographics (Tier 1) had a Tjur's D of 1.52. Adding pre-service sexual assault to the birth demographics model differentiated these groups by an additional 3.54 percentage points, as shown by the change in Tjur's D in the adjusted model (Table 4.2), for a total difference of 5.1 percentage points. Specifically, although the baseline risk of sexual assault for all women in the military was 4.9 percent, the average predicted risk of sexual assault for a model including birth demographics and pre-service sexual assault was approximately 9.7 percent among women who experienced a sexual assault and 4.6 percent among women with no past-year sexual assault.

Unlike other sexual assault risk factors that we discuss in this report, pre-service sexual assault was assessed retrospectively on the same survey as the sexual assault outcome measure. As discussed in Chapter Two, the mechanisms that create the association between recent (past-year) sexual assaults and earlier sexual assaults are not well known, and the various proposed mechanisms lead to very different interpretations of that association. The association may occur, in part, because there are risk factors outside of this model that explain why some individuals were at high risk both in the pre-service period and the past year; it may occur, in part, because early sexual assaults affect victims in ways that increase their risk of future assaults; and it may also be, in part, a measurement artifact. For example, the two assessments share response biases that may inflate the correlation between them, and reporting past-year sexual assault experiences on the survey may alter whether respondents remember, and how they understand, their pre-service experiences. In contrast, the other factors in these models were assessed prospectively and using official records, so they do not generally have these same difficulties in interpretation.[1]

---

[1]   Given the possibility that our retrospective, survey-based measure of pre-service sexual assault may partially reflect characteristics about the service member at the time of the RMWS survey (in addition to information about the person's pre-service sexual assault experiences), it may be inappropriate to treat this as a characteristic that existed at time of entry into service. Specifically, it may not be appropriate to control for this factor when producing effect sizes for factors in Tiers 2, 3, or 4. To investigate this concern, we reran the Tier 2, 3, and 4 models

Table 4.2
Tier 2: Association Between Characteristics at Entry and Past-Year Sexual Assault, Women

Risk Factor	Bivariate			Adjusted for Prior Tiers			Adjusted, Including Current Tier	
	Risk Ratio (95% CI)	p-value	Tjur's D	Adjusted Risk Ratio (95% CI)	p-value	Δ Tjur's D	Adjusted Risk Ratio (95% CI)	p-value
AFQT score (10 points)[a]	1.21 (1.17–1.25)	0.00	0.49	1.18 (1.14–1.22)	0.00	0.45	1.11 (1.08–1.15)	0.00
Missing	0.30 (0.12–0.75)	0.01	0.02	0.57 (0.27–1.19)	0.13	0.01	0.81 (0.43–1.56)	0.54
Pre-service sexual assault	4.47 (3.97–5.03)	0.00	2.79	4.40 (3.92–4.93)	0.00	3.54	3.98 (3.54–4.47)	0.00
Service branch		0.00	0.54		0.00	0.45		0.00
Army	1.61 (1.44–1.81)			1.73 (1.54–1.95)			1.74 (1.55–1.96)	
Navy	2.23 (1.95–2.55)			2.03 (1.78–2.33)			1.85 (1.62–2.10)	
Air Force	1 (reference)			1 (reference)			1 (reference)	
Marine Corps	2.71 (2.26–3.24)			2.08 (1.73–2.49)			1.96 (1.65–2.33)	
Entry type		0.00	0.23		0.00	0.04		0.00
Enlisted[b]	1 (reference)			1 (reference)			1 (reference)	
Officer, academy	0.77 (0.60–0.98)			0.84 (0.66–1.08)			0.95 (0.74–1.21)	
Officer, ROTC	0.58 (0.48–0.70)			0.74 (0.61–0.89)			0.77 (0.64–0.93)	

Table 4.2—Continued

| Risk Factor | Bivariate | | | Adjusted for Prior Tiers | | | Adjusted, Including Current Tier | |
	Risk Ratio (95% CI)	p-value	Tjur's D	Adjusted Risk Ratio (95% CI)	p-value	Δ Tjur's D	Adjusted Risk Ratio (95% CI)	p-value
Officer, other	0.33 (0.26–0.41)			0.62 (0.49–0.79)			0.62 (0.49–0.79)	

NOTE: We scaled Tjur's D by a factor of 100 to put it on a percentage-point scale.

[a] AFQT scores are for enlisted members only.

[b] Enlisted includes warrant officers and those who went through Officer Candidate School.

AFQT score and branch of service were the next-best predictors of sexual assault risk among the characteristics at entry that we studied. For enlisted members, better scores on the AFQT were associated with higher risk of past-year sexual assault. Specifically, with each increase of 10 percentile points on the test, risk of past-year sexual assault was elevated by a factor between 1.11 in the *adjusted, including current tier* model and 1.21 in the bivariate model. As we noted in earlier volumes in this series, branch of service is a strong predictor of sexual assault risk: Women in the Air Force have significantly lower risk of past-year sexual assaults than those in the other DoD services. Finally, in this analysis, members entering service as officers generally had a lower risk of sexual assault than did enlisted members.

AFQT and branch of service each improved upon the models that included only birth demographics by a Tjur's D of approximately 0.5 percentage points. Whereas women's overall average risk of sexual assault was 4.9 percent, predicted risk of sexual assault from a model including both tiers of factors averaged 10.4 percent for women who experienced a sexual assault in the past year and 4.6 percent for those who did not. This corresponds to a Tjur's D of 5.85 percentage points, which is a large increase over the Tjur's D for the model that included only the birth demographics from Tier 1 (the change in Tjur's D between the two models is 4.33).

Personal and Career History

Table 4.3 provides effect size estimates for the personal history and career history factors of service women. As before, bivariate models show the association between each factor and past-year sexual assault, and the *adjusted for prior tiers* models show the association between each factor and past-year sexual assault after controlling for all factors from Tiers 1 and 2 (i.e., birth demographics and characteristics at entry). The *adjusted, including current tier* analyses presented in Table 4.3 were calculated as separate models for personal history and career history factors. These estimates for personal history factors controlled for all personal history factors in this tier, plus the factors from earlier tiers of the analysis, but they did not control for the career history factors. Similarly, these estimates for the career history factors controlled for all career history factors in this tier, as well as factors from earlier tiers, but not for the personal history factors.

Among the personal history factors, being single, having fewer dependents, and having never attended college all appear to be associated with increased risk of sexual

---

excluding pre-service sexual assault. The multivariate risk ratios for each predictor did not change meaningfully within the level of precision used in this report. Additionally, these alternative models had the same pattern of significant effects as we present in our primary analysis, except for two marginally significant organizational demographics in Tier 4. Finally, the Tjur's D fit for the model including all of the other risk factors across all tiers improved by 3.78 percentage points when pre-service sexual assault was included, an amount nearly equivalent to the contribution that pre-service sexual assault made when controlling for only birth demographics (3.54 percentage points). This implies that our measure of pre-service sexual assault was not strongly associated with the important predictors in Tiers 2, 3, and 4.

Table 4.3
Tier 3: Association Between Personal and Career History and Past-Year Sexual Assault, Women

Risk Factor	Bivariate			Adjusted for Prior Tiers			Adjusted, Including Current Tier	
	Risk Ratio (95% CI)	p-value	Tjur's D	Adjusted Risk Ratio (95% CI)	p-value	Δ Tjur's D	Adjusted Risk Ratio (95% CI)	p-value
Personal history								
Marital status (single)	2.23 (2.05–2.43)	0.00	0.68	1.63 (1.50–1.79)	0.00	0.38	1.71 (1.55–1.89)	0.00
Number of dependents	0.73 (0.70–0.76)	0.00	0.46	0.93 (0.89–0.98)	0.00	0.03	1.05 (1.00–1.11)	0.04
Educational attainment		0.00	0.75		0.00	0.07		0.00
Up to high school diploma	1 (reference)			1 (reference)			1 (reference)	
Some college	0.45 (0.39–0.51)			0.76 (0.66–0.87)			0.76 (0.66–0.87)	
Bachelor's degree	0.54 (0.48–0.61)			0.86 (0.74–1.00)			0.84 (0.72–0.97)	
Graduate degree	0.24 (0.19–0.29)			0.68 (0.52–0.89)			0.67 (0.51–0.87)	
Missing	0.83 (0.65–1.03)			1.11 (0.84–1.43)			1.06 (0.81–1.37)	
Career history								
Pay grade		0.00	1.16		0.00	0.11		0.06
E1–E3	1.25 (1.14–1.37)			1.07 (0.97–1.18)			1.08 (0.98–1.20)	
E4	1 (reference)			1 (reference)			1 (reference)	

Table 4.3—Continued

Risk Factor	Bivariate			Adjusted for Prior Tiers			Adjusted, Including Current Tier	
	Risk Ratio (95% CI)	p-value	Tjur's D	Adjusted Risk Ratio (95% CI)	p-value	Δ Tjur's D	Adjusted Risk Ratio (95% CI)	p-value
E5–E6	0.53 (0.47–0.59)			0.80 (0.70–0.90)			0.85 (0.74–0.98)	
E7–E9	0.26 (0.20–0.32)			0.64 (0.48–0.83)			0.73 (0.54–0.97)	
O1–O3	0.55 (0.48–0.63)			1.04 (0.78–1.37)			1.11 (0.75–1.61)	
O4–O6	0.20 (0.14–0.26)			0.77 (0.49–1.17)			0.90 (0.53–1.49)	
W1–W5	0.48 (0.29–0.75)			1.04 (0.61–1.66)			1.19 (0.64–2.07)	
Promotion speed (years)	1.03 (1.01–1.04)	0.00	0.02	0.96 (0.94–0.98)	0.00	0.06	0.97 (0.95–0.99)	0.01
Past deployment (2001–2013) (years)	0.66 (0.61–0.70)	0.00	0.31	0.98 (0.91–1.05)	0.54	0.00	0.99 (0.92–1.07)	0.81
Occupation group (enlisted)		0.00	0.49		0.00	0.27		0.00
Infantry, gun crews, and seamanship specialists	0.87 (0.70–1.07)			1.04 (0.84–1.28)			1.05 (0.84–1.29)	
Electronic equipment repairers	0.88 (0.75–1.04)			0.84 (0.71–0.99)			0.87 (0.73–1.02)	
Communications and intelligence specialists	0.81 (0.70–0.94)			0.79 (0.68–0.92)			0.82 (0.70–0.96)	
Health care specialists	0.60 (0.52–0.69)			0.73 (0.63–0.85)			0.72 (0.62–0.84)	

Table 4.3—Continued

Risk Factor	Bivariate			Adjusted for Prior Tiers			Adjusted, Including Current Tier	
	Risk Ratio (95% CI)	p-value	Tjur's D	Adjusted Risk Ratio (95% CI)	p-value	Δ Tjur's D	Adjusted Risk Ratio (95% CI)	p-value
Other technical and allied specialists	0.74 (0.57–0.95)			0.93 (0.70–1.20)			0.95 (0.72–1.24)	
Functional support and administration	0.59 (0.52–0.68)			0.89 (0.77–1.02)			0.90 (0.78–1.03)	
Electrical/mechanical equipment repairers	1 (reference)			1 (reference)			1 (reference)	
Craftsworkers	1.01 (0.79–1.28)			1.20 (0.93–1.53)			1.20 (0.93–1.53)	
Service and supply handlers	0.75 (0.64–0.87)			1.06 (0.91–1.24)			1.07 (0.91–1.25)	
Nonoccupational	0.65 (0.47–0.88)			0.54 (0.39–0.74)			0.53 (0.38–0.73)	
Occupation group (officer)								
Tactical operations officers	1 (reference)			1 (reference)			1 (reference)	
Intelligence officers	1.02 (0.67–1.52)			1.07 (0.70–1.62)			1.05 (0.68–1.58)	
Engineering and maintenance officers	0.85 (0.56–1.26)			0.87 (0.57–1.30)			0.84 (0.55–1.27)	
Scientists and professionals	0.72 (0.44–1.13)			0.87 (0.51–1.42)			0.90 (0.53–1.47)	
Health care officers	0.31 (0.21–0.45)			0.44 (0.28–0.68)			0.44 (0.29–0.69)	

Table 4.3—Continued

| Risk Factor | Bivariate | | | Adjusted for Prior Tiers | | | Adjusted, Including Current Tier | |
	Risk Ratio (95% CI)	p-value	Tjur's D	Adjusted Risk Ratio (95% CI)	p-value	Δ Tjur's D	Adjusted Risk Ratio (95% CI)	p-value
Administrators	0.75 (0.51–1.11)			0.90 (0.60–1.35)			0.86 (0.57–1.29)	
Supply, procurement, and allied officers	0.66 (0.43–1.00)			0.76 (0.48–1.16)			0.74 (0.47–1.13)	
Other	1.26 (0.77–1.99)			0.83 (0.50–1.33)			0.86 (0.52–1.37)	

NOTE: We scaled Tjur's D by a factor of 100 to put it on a percentage-point scale.

assault in all models. However, the change in Tjur's D for educational attainment and number of dependents in the adjusted models was substantially lower than each factor's Tjur's D in the bivariate analyses. This indicates that much of the explanatory power of the factors' association with sexual assault risk results from their correlations with factors in earlier model tiers, particularly age, race, and service branch.

Although all the career history factors had a significant bivariate association with past-year sexual assault, the factor representing past deployments between September 11, 2001, and July 2013 was not significant after adjusting the association to account for factors in prior tiers, and pay grade was no longer significant when controlling for both prior tiers and other career history factors. The promotion speed factor was measured relative to other service members in the same pay grade, with higher values indicating faster promotion. Therefore, this factor shows that faster promotion was significantly associated with lower sexual assault risk. Across all models, enlisted women in communications and intelligence, health care, and electronic equipment repair occupations had significantly reduced risk compared with women in some other occupations, including electrical/mechanical equipment repairers. Similarly, the nonoccupational category (which includes patients, students, trainees, and prisoners) had significantly lower risk than the electrical/mechanical repairers that served as the reference group.

Among officers, after accounting for all career history and earlier-tier factors, only officers with health care occupations had significantly lower risk of sexual assault than tactical operations officers, the reference group. The difference was large, however: Health care officers had less than half the risk of a past-year sexual assault than tactical operations officers had.

The predicted risk of sexual assault for a model that included all three tiers of factors averaged 11.2 percent for women who experienced a sexual assault in the past year and 4.5 percent for those who did not. This corresponds to a Tjur's D of 6.70 percentage points, which is a small 0.85–percentage point improvement relative to a model with only Tier 1 and 2 risk factors. This small change reflects the modest effect sizes for most of the factors in this tier relative to some of the factors in Tiers 1 and 2.

Recent Experiences

Table 4.4 provides results for the past-year risk factors, those closest in time to the period over which their sexual assault experiences are reported. These risk factors are presented in three subgroups: recent history, past-year organizational unit, and separation from the military. As before, results from the *adjusted for prior tiers* models controlled for all factors in previous tiers but not for other factors in this tier (Tier 4). The *adjusted, including current tier* results controlled for factors in previous tiers and other factors in the same subgroup within Tier 4. For instance, the risk ratio reported for the deployed in the past 12 months factor controlled for factors in Tiers 1, 2, and 3, as well as the factors labeled as recent history, such as OCONUS service and service on a ship. However, the model did not control for the factors in the past-year organizational characteristics subgroup, even though they are in the same tier.

Table 4.4
Tier 4: Association Between Recent Experiences and Past-Year Sexual Assault, Women

Risk Factor	Bivariate			Adjusted for Prior Tiers			Adjusted, Including Current Tier	
	Risk Ratio (95% CI)	p-value	Tjur's D	Risk Ratio (95% CI)	p-value	Δ Tjur's D	Risk Ratio (95% CI)	p-value
Recent history								
Deployed in the past 12 months	1.42 (1.15–1.75)	0.00	0.05	1.46 (1.20–1.78)	0.00	0.09	1.38 (1.14–1.68)	0.00
Location (OCONUS)	1.19 (1.05–1.36)	0.01	0.03	1.12 (0.99–1.27)	0.07	0.03	1.12 (0.99–1.27)	0.08
Assigned to a ship (past 12 months)	2.15 (1.73–2.68)	0.00	0.29	1.45 (1.15–1.83)	0.00	0.11	1.32 (1.05–1.67)	0.02
Past-year organizational characteristics								
Unit identification code								
Number of personnel (per 1,000)	1.40 (1.28–1.53)	0.00	0.44	1.09 (0.99–1.21)	0.08	0.10	1.08 (0.98–1.20)	0.14
Average age (years)	0.90 (0.89–0.91)	0.00	0.75	0.99 (0.97–1.00)	0.13	0.03	0.99 (0.98–1.01)	0.37
Percentage male (10 points)	1.21 (1.17–1.26)	0.00	0.25	1.07 (1.02–1.13)	0.00	0.05	1.09 (1.03–1.15)	0.00
Percentage male leadership (10 points)	1.06 (1.03–1.09)	0.00	0.04	1.02 (0.99–1.05)	0.21	0.01	1.04 (1.00–1.07)	0.05
Postal code								
Number of personnel (per 10,000)	1.03 (0.99–1.07)	0.19	0.00	1.01 (0.96–1.06)	0.67	0.00	0.99 (0.93–1.05)	0.68
Average age (years)	0.87 (0.85–0.90)	0.00	0.51	0.97 (0.94–0.99)	0.02	0.07	0.97 (0.95–1.00)	0.06

Risk Factor	Bivariate			Adjusted for Prior Tiers			Adjusted, Including Current Tier	
	Risk Ratio (95% CI)	p-value	Tjur's D	Risk Ratio (95% CI)	p-value	Δ Tjur's D	Risk Ratio (95% CI)	p-value
Percentage male (10 points)	1.29 (1.18–1.42)	0.00	0.13	1.11 (1.00–1.24)	0.04	0.04	1.08 (0.96–1.21)	0.22
Percentage male leadership (10 points)	1.04 (0.92–1.17)	0.53	0.00	0.95 (0.86–1.05)	0.32	0.01	0.98 (0.88–1.09)	0.70
Major command code (or monitored command code for the Marine Corps)								
Number of personnel (per 10,000)	1.01 (1.01–1.02)	0.00	0.04	1.02 (1.01–1.02)	0.00	0.07	1.01 (1.00–1.02)	0.00
Average age (years)	0.86 (0.85–0.88)	0.00	0.64	0.96 (0.94–0.99)	0.00	0.07	0.99 (0.96–1.01)	0.29
Percentage male (10 points)	1.42 (1.31–1.54)	0.00	0.22	1.16 (1.05–1.30)	0.01	0.04	1.09 (0.96–1.25)	0.17
Percentage male leadership (10 points)	1.49 (1.29–1.72)	0.00	0.10	1.07 (0.93–1.22)	0.35	0.01	1.12 (0.95–1.31)	0.17
Separated from the military								
Separated from military	1.85 (1.15–2.98)	0.01	0.03	2.12 (1.26–3.59)	0.01	0.02	2.12 (1.26–3.59)	0.01

NOTE: We scaled Tjur's D by a factor of 100 to put it on a percentage-point scale.

Women who were deployed, served overseas, or served on a ship in the past year were all more likely to have been sexually assaulted in the past year, according to the bivariate results. However, once conceptually prior factors were accounted for, serving overseas was no longer a significant predictor of risk, and the effect of serving on a ship was substantially attenuated. Still, even in the *adjusted, including current tier* estimates, both being deployed in the past 12 months and being assigned to a ship in the past 12 months were associated with more than 30-percent elevations in risk for women. Nevertheless, these factors had modest explanatory power over risk after accounting for conceptually prior factors, as demonstrated by changes in Tjur's D in the adjusted models of about one-tenth of a percentage point.

For the characteristics of the organizations in which women served, we examined three levels of organization: unit, using the unit identification code; installation, using the postal code of the service members' duty unit, which is a proxy for the installation where the member is assigned; and major command, using the major command code for service members in the Army, Navy, and Air Force, or the monitored command code for service members in the Marine Corps. Each organizational level was estimated in a separate model for the *adjusted, including current tier* estimates.

In the bivariate model, the average age of other members of the organization and the percentage who were men were significantly associated with sexual assault risk for all levels of the organization. Specifically, women working in groups that were older and that had a higher percentage of women faced lower risks of sexual assault. The number of people in the organization and the difference in the percentage of men in the organization's leadership relative to in the full population of the organization were also significant for the unit and major command levels of analysis, but not for the installation (or postal code) level. Moreover, after controlling for conceptually prior risk factors, only percentage male in the organization remained significant for all three organizational levels.

In the *adjusted, including current tier* estimates, few factors related to organizational characteristics remained as significant predictors. Thus, some of the predictive power of the percentage male factor observed in the adjusted analyses was shared with other organizational factors. Indeed, when we removed number of personnel in the organization from the model (not shown in the table), percentage male was again a significant predictor of risk at the unit and major command levels, and overall model fit was barely affected. The risk ratios for the percentage male effect were quite large and were nearly identical across the three organizational levels, although only one was statistically significant. In each case, as the percentage of the organization that was male increased by 10 percentage points, the risk of sexual assault to women rose by about 9 percentage points.

The final subgroup of factors we examined included a single factor indicating whether the respondent left the military between the time the survey sample was drawn (April 2014) and the end of the survey field period (September 2014). This factor was significant in bivariate models and models adjusting for prior tiers. (Because there were no other factors in this subgroup, the *adjusted, including current tier* estimate was the same as the *adjusted for prior tiers* estimate.) The risk ratio for the adjusted effect was large, suggesting that women who left the military recently had more than twice the risk of having had a past-year sexual assault than those who remained in the military. This effect controlled for age, rank, and several other factors likely to be associated with leaving the military, so it cannot be explained by the fact that, for instance, more-junior personnel departed the military in any given year than more-senior personnel. It is worth noting when interpreting this effect that the causal effect could run the opposite direction as implied by the model. The separated from military factor assesses an event that could have occurred after the sexual assault. Although it is possible that the period immediately before and after separating from the military is one of especially high risk, it is also possible that past-year sexual assaults increase the likelihood of separating from the military or that some third factor is associated with both the risk of assault and the likelihood of separating.

As noted, in the RMWS, the average past-year sexual assault risk for women in the military was 4.9 percent. The predicted risk of sexual assault from the final model that included all four tiers of factors averaged 11.7 percent for women who experienced a sexual assault in the past year and 4.5 percent for those who did not. This corresponds to a Tjur's D of 7.17 percentage points, which is a small (0.47–percentage point) improvement over the model with only the factors from Tiers 1, 2, and 3. Thus, it appears that most of the predictive power of our set of potential risk factors among women comes from birth demographics and characteristics at the time of service entry rather than from personal and career history or recent military experiences.

Sexual Assault Risk Factors for Service Men

The next set of analyses addresses the sexual assault risk factors for service men. Using the same procedures as for women, we first assess the association between birth demographic risk factors and past-year sexual assault (Tier 1), then consider characteristics at the time of service entry (Tier 2), personal and career history (Tier 3), and recent experiences (Tier 4).

Birth Demographics

Table 4.5 displays the bivariate and multivariate association between birth demographics (age and race) and past-year sexual assaults of men. As was true for women, age was significantly associated with risk of sexual assault. Each additional ten years of age was associated with more than a 40-percent reduction in risk of sexual assault. No statistically significant associations were found for race, however.

Results from the RMWS indicated that the average risk of past-year sexual assault for active-duty service men was 0.9 percent, meaning that if we knew nothing about

Table 4.5
Tier 1: Association Between Birth Demographics and Past-Year Sexual Assault, Men

	Bivariate			Adjusted, Including Current Tier	
Risk Factor	Risk Ratio (95% CI)	*p*-value	Tjur's D	Adjusted Risk Ratio (95% CI)	*p*-value
Age (decades)	0.57 (0.43–0.75)	0.00	0.14	0.57 (0.44–0.75)	0.00
Race		0.24	0.05		0.24
Asian	1.07 (0.47–2.45)			1.09 (0.47–2.49)	
Black	1.64 (1.02–2.62)			1.69 (1.06–2.70)	
Hispanic	1.29 (0.66–2.53)			1.24 (0.63–2.42)	
Other	1.81 (0.75–4.37)			1.62 (0.67–3.95)	
White	1 (reference)			1 (reference)	

NOTE: We scaled Tjur's D by a factor of 100 to put it on a percentage-point scale. Because there are no earlier tiers for Tier 1, the bivariate and adjusted effect sizes are identical.

men in the service who had and had not been sexually assaulted, we would estimate that members of both groups faced a risk of 0.9 percent. The predicted risk of sexual assault from a model that included both age and race averaged approximately 1.1 percent for men who experienced a sexual assault in the past year and 0.9 percent for those who did not. This results in a Tjur's D of 0.20 percentage points for this model.

Characteristics at the Time of Service Entry

Table 4.6 provides associations between the Tier 2 characteristics at service entry and past-year sexual assaults of men. As was the case for women, pre-service sexual assaults were a significant risk factor for individual men, and this factor explained a large portion of population risk. Men who were categorized as having been sexually assaulted before entering the military were more than 16 times as likely to report experiencing a past-year sexual assault, after controlling for other characteristics at entry and Tier 1 factors. Moreover, adding pre-service sexual assaults to a risk model that included just Tier 1 factors improved the differentiation in average risk of those who were and were not assaulted by approximately 2.5 percentage points.

Enlisted men's AFQT scores predicted sexual assault risk better than the Tier 1 birth demographics did but did not remain a significant predictor when other Tier 2 factors were included in the model.

Table 4.6
Tier 2: Association Between Characteristics at Entry and Past-Year Sexual Assaults, Men

Risk Factor	Bivariate			Adjusted for Prior Tiers			Adjusted, Including Current Tier	
	Risk Ratio (95% CI)	p-value	Tjur's D	Adjusted Risk Ratio (95% CI)	p-value	Δ Tjur's D	Adjusted Risk Ratio (95% CI)	p-value
AFQT score (10 points)[a]	1.12 (1.00–1.26)	0.05	0.04	1.15 (1.01–1.31)	0.03	0.06	1.11 (0.99–1.25)	0.13
Missing	0.26 (0.03–2.17)	0.21	0.00	0.41 (0.08–2.25)	0.31	0.00	0.55 (0.13–2.32)	0.42
Pre-service sexual assault	18.56 (11.38–30.25)	0.00	1.97	17.95 (11.46–28.12)	0.00	2.45	16.25 (9.89–26.69)	0.00
Service branch		0.00	0.18		0.00	0.20		0.00
Army	3.26 (2.19–4.87)			3.29 (2.19–4.96)			3.25 (2.17–4.86)	
Navy	5.11 (3.19–8.18)			4.93 (3.14–7.73)			4.53 (2.87–7.15)	
Air Force	1 (reference)			1 (reference)			1 (reference)	
Marine Corps	3.91 (2.19–6.96)			3.26 (1.82–5.86)			3.21 (1.88–5.51)	
Entry type		0.00	0.05		0.00	0.02		0.00
Enlisted[b]	1 (reference)			1 (reference)			1 (reference)	
Officer, academy	0.30 (0.15–0.63)			0.39 (0.19–0.82)			0.42 (0.20–0.88)	
Officer, ROTC	0.42 (0.26–0.68)			0.59 (0.37–0.94)			0.66 (0.41–1.06)	

Table 4.6—Continued

Risk Factor	Bivariate			Adjusted for Prior Tiers			Adjusted, Including Current Tier	
	Risk Ratio (95% CI)	p-value	Tjur's D	Adjusted Risk Ratio (95% CI)	p-value	Δ Tjur's D	Adjusted Risk Ratio (95% CI)	p-value
Officer, other	0.20 (0.07–0.54)			0.34 (0.13–0.94)			0.27 (0.10–0.76)	

NOTE: We scaled Tjur's D by a factor of 100 to put it on a percentage-point scale.

[a] AFQT scores are for enlisted members only.

[b] Enlisted includes warrant officers and those who went through Officer Candidate School.

Service branch and entry type were also significantly associated with sexual assault risk while controlling for Tier 1 and other Tier 2 risk factors. Moreover, the risk ratios associated with each were large. When controlling for birth demographics and other Tier 2 factors, men who entered the Army, Navy, and Marine Corps had between about 3 and 4.5 times the risk of a past-year sexual assault as men who entered the Air Force. Similarly, members who entered the service as officers had approximately half the risk as those who entered as enlisted.

Whereas the RMWS estimated that 0.9 percent of all active-duty men in the military were sexually assaulted in the past year, the predicted risk of sexual assault from a model that included Tier 2 factors in addition to Tier 1 factors averaged 3.8 percent for men who experienced a sexual assault in the past year and 0.9 percent for those who did not. This corresponds to a Tjur's D of 2.86 percentage points, which is a large 2.66–percentage point improvement over the model with only Tier 1 factors.

Personal and Career History

Tier 3 includes two subgroups of factors, personal history and career history, which are evaluated in separate models when producing *adjusted, including current tier* estimates (Table 4.7). Marital status (single) and number of dependents were the only personal history factors that significantly improved upon models that included only the factors in Tiers 1 and 2. When controlling for age or other conceptually prior factors, being single was associated with 1.50 times the risk of past-year sexual assaults of men in comparison with men who indicated other marital statuses. However, in the *adjusted, including current tier* estimates, which added marital status, number of dependents, and educational attainment, neither marital status nor number of dependents remained statistically significant. This is likely because being single and having fewer dependents were highly associated with each other, and this did not uniquely explain sexual assault risk.

Among career history factors, only pay grade significantly improved upon the model with all Tier 1 and Tier 2 factors in it. Specifically, compared with the E4 pay grade, service men in E5–E6, E7–E8, O1–O3, and W1–W5 all had substantially lower risk of sexual assault. For instance, when controlling for Tier 1 and Tier 2 factors, E4 men had almost six times the risk of sexual assault as men who were warrant officers had. Moreover, the effect remained significant in the model controlling for other career history factors.

Together, the personal history and career history factors in Tier 3 modestly improved upon the model using Tier 1 and Tier 2 factors. The predicted risk of sexual assault from a model that included factors from Tiers 1, 2, and 3 averaged 4.2 percent for men who experienced a sexual assault in the past year and 0.9 percent for those who did not. This corresponds to a Tjur's D of 3.27 percentage points, which is a 0.41–percentage point improvement over the model with only Tier 1 and Tier 2 factors.

Table 4.7
Tier 3: Association Between Personal and Career History and Past-Year Sexual Assault, Men

Risk Factor	Bivariate			Adjusted for Prior Tiers			Adjusted, Including Current Tier	
	Risk Ratio (95% CI)	p-value	Tjur's D	Adjusted Risk Ratio (95% CI)	p-value	Δ Tjur's D	Adjusted Risk Ratio (95% CI)	p-value
Personal history								
Marital status (single)	2.01 (1.40–2.89)	0.00	0.12	1.50 (1.05–2.16)	0.03	−0.13	1.43 (0.89–2.32)	0.14
Number of dependents	0.78 (0.70–0.88)	0.00	0.11	0.89 (0.80–1.00)	0.05	0.02	0.97 (0.84–1.12)	0.68
Educational attainment		0.00	0.10		0.84	−0.01		0.79
Up to high school diploma	1 (reference)			1 (reference)			1 (reference)	
Some college	0.49 (0.19–1.24)			0.75 (0.26–2.23)			0.76 (0.26–2.25)	
Bachelor's degree	0.69 (0.44–1.09)			1.00 (0.58–1.72)			0.96 (0.55–1.66)	
Graduate degree	0.26 (0.15–0.43)			0.79 (0.40–1.59)			0.76 (0.38–1.52)	
Missing	0.42 (0.14–1.24)			0.60 (0.21–1.74)			0.57 (0.20–1.61)	
Career history								
Pay grade		0.00	0.22		0.00	0.16		0.01
E1–E3	0.89 (0.51–1.55)			0.87 (0.50–1.52)			0.85 (0.51–1.44)	
E4	1 (reference)			1 (reference)			1 (reference)	

Table 4.7—Continued

Risk Factor	Bivariate			Adjusted for Prior Tiers			Adjusted, Including Current Tier	
	Risk Ratio (95% CI)	p-value	Tjur's D	Adjusted Risk Ratio (95% CI)	p-value	Δ Tjur's D	Adjusted Risk Ratio (95% CI)	p-value
E5–E6	0.55 (0.36–0.84)			0.62 (0.41–0.95)			0.70 (0.44–1.12)	
E7–E9	0.20 (0.12–0.35)			0.27 (0.14–0.51)			0.31 (0.15–0.63)	
O1–O3	0.24 (0.14–0.41)			0.31 (0.14–0.65)			0.34 (0.13–0.89)	
O4–O6	0.23 (0.12–0.44)			0.32 (0.10–1.07)			0.37 (0.09–1.61)	
W1–W5	0.14 (0.05–0.39)			0.17 (0.06–0.50)			0.22 (0.06–0.79)	
Promotion speed (years)	1.03 (0.99–1.08)	0.19	0.00	0.98 (0.93–1.03)	0.36	0.02	1.00 (0.94–1.06)	0.97
Past deployment (years)	0.69 (0.56–0.86)	0.00	0.08	0.82 (0.66–1.03)	0.09	0.06	0.86 (0.69–1.08)	0.20
Occupation group (enlisted)		0.09	0.17		0.11	0.38		0.12
Infantry, gun crews, and seamanship specialists	1.11 (0.57–2.17)			1.06 (0.57–1.97)			1.07 (0.58–1.99)	
Electronic equipment repairers	1.03 (0.48–2.17)			0.81 (0.37–1.75)			0.80 (0.37–1.75)	
Communication and intelligence specialists	0.46 (0.24–0.89)			0.45 (0.23–0.88)			0.46 (0.23–0.91)	
Health care specialists	0.90 (0.47–1.73)			0.78 (0.39–1.58)			0.75 (0.37–1.50)	

Table 4.7—Continued

Risk Factor	Bivariate			Adjusted for Prior Tiers			Adjusted, Including Current Tier	
	Risk Ratio (95% CI)	p-value	Tjur's D	Adjusted Risk Ratio (95% CI)	p-value	Δ Tjur's D	Adjusted Risk Ratio (95% CI)	p-value
Other technical and allied specialists	0.63 (0.26–1.52)			0.66 (0.29–1.53)			0.64 (0.28–1.50)	
Functional support and administration	1.33 (0.68–2.61)			1.41 (0.69–2.88)			1.42 (0.7–2.87)	
Electrical/mechanical equipment repairers	1 (reference)			1 (reference)			1 (reference)	
Craftsworkers	0.47 (0.18–1.27)			0.54 (0.20–1.44)			0.52 (0.19–1.41)	
Service and supply handlers	1.01 (0.51–1.99)			1.44 (0.74–2.80)			1.43 (0.74–2.79)	
Nonoccupational	0.22 (0.07–0.77)			0.21 (0.06–0.76)			0.22 (0.06–0.80)	
Occupation group (officer)	1 (reference)			1 (reference)			1 (reference)	
Tactical operations officers	1.06 (0.32–3.56)			1.04 (0.30–3.59)			1.00 (0.28–3.51)	
Intelligence officers	0.73 (0.31–1.70)			0.78 (0.33–1.85)			0.81 (0.35–1.86)	
Engineering and maintenance officers	0.76 (0.15–3.87)			1.09 (0.25–4.74)			0.93 (0.21–4.19)	
Scientists and professionals	0.47 (0.16–1.40)			0.70 (0.22–2.20)			0.62 (0.19–1.99)	
Health care officers	1.15 (0.28–4.75)			1.15 (0.27–4.84)			1.11 (0.27–4.67)	

Table 4.7—Continued

Risk Factor	Bivariate			Adjusted for Prior Tiers			Adjusted, Including Current Tier	
	Risk Ratio (95% CI)	*p*-value	Tjur's D	Adjusted Risk Ratio (95% CI)	*p*-value	Δ Tjur's D	Adjusted Risk Ratio (95% CI)	*p*-value
Administrators	1.34 (0.51–3.57)			1.16 (0.42–3.20)			1.16 (0.42–3.19)	
Supply, procurement, and allied officers	0.28 (0.04–2.07)			0.21 (0.03–1.61)			0.24 (0.03–1.77)	
Other	1 (reference)			1 (reference)			1 (reference)	

NOTE: We scaled Tjur's D by a factor of 100 to put it on a percentage-point scale.

Recent Experiences

As noted earlier, Tier 4 factors are divided into three subgroups: recent history, past-year organizational characteristics, and separation from the military (Table 4.8). We evaluated each subgroup in a separate model to produce the *adjusted, including current tier* estimates. Among recent history factors, only serving overseas in the past year (OCONUS location) significantly predicted sexual assault risk when controlling for all Tier 1–3 factors. Moreover, the point estimate for the risk ratio was fairly large, suggesting that men serving oversees in the past year were 1.62 times more likely to be sexually assaulted than those serving in CONUS. Although the point estimate remained fairly large for the *adjusted, including current tier* estimate, this factor was no longer statistically significant, because this factor was associated with other risk factors added into the model. Those factors were (1) being deployed in the past 12 months and (2) being assigned to a ship in the past 12 months.

For the characteristics of the organizations in which men served, we examined three levels of organization: unit, installation (based on postal code), and major command. Few of these organizational characteristics were significantly associated with sexual assault risk for men, even in bivariate analyses. One exception was that a higher average age of others in the organization was associated with reduced risk of sexual assault for all three organizational levels. However, when controlling for factors in Tiers 1–3, average age remained a significant predictor only for major commands. At that level, for each additional year in the average age of personnel in the command, the risk of sexual assault to men in the command declined by a factor of 0.92.

Finally, we also investigated the association between separation from service and sexual assault risk. When controlling for factors in Tiers 1–3, active-duty men who separated from the military between the time the survey sample was drawn and the end of the fielding period were almost five times more likely to have been sexually assaulted in the past year than men who did not separate during that interval. As we noted earlier for women, this should not be interpreted as a true, predictive risk factor, because the separation likely occurred after the sexual assault, not before. However, it suggests that the association between sexual assault risk and separation is not explained by any of the other factors in Tiers 1–3.

The predicted risk of sexual assault from a model that included factors from all four tiers averaged approximately 5.4 percent for men who experienced a sexual assault in the past year and 0.9 percent for those who did not. Thus, the model successfully identified individuals who experienced these assaults by estimating that their risk was five times greater than the risk of men who did not experience an assault. This risk differentiation corresponds to a Tjur's D of 4.46 percentage points, a relatively large (1.19–percentage point) improvement over a model with only Tier 1–3 factors.

Table 4.8
Tier 4: Association Between Recent Experiences and Past-Year Sexual Assault, Men

Risk Factor	Bivariate			Adjusted for Prior Tiers			Adjusted, Including Current Tier	
	Risk Ratio (95% CI)	p-value	Tjur's D	Risk Ratio (95% CI)	p-value	Δ Tjur's D	Risk Ratio (95% CI)	p-value
Recent history								
Deployed in the past 12 months	0.72 (0.44–1.19)	0.20	0.01	0.73 (0.44–1.22)	0.23	0.03	0.72 (0.43–1.19)	0.20
Location (OCONUS)	1.83 (1.15–2.92)	0.01	0.08	1.62 (1.02–2.59)	0.04	0.23	1.54 (0.94–2.52)	0.09
Assigned to a ship (past 12 months)	2.96 (1.59–5.51)	0.00	0.14	1.85 (0.91–3.76)	0.09	0.08	1.77 (0.84–3.76)	0.14
Past-year organizational characteristics								
Unit identification code								
Number of personnel (per 1,000)	1.22 (0.95–1.57)	0.12	0.02	0.89 (0.62–1.27)	0.52	0.02	0.84 (0.58–1.22)	0.36
Average age (years)	0.92 (0.88–0.95)	0.00	0.09	0.97 (0.93–1.01)	0.19	0.02	0.96 (0.92–1.01)	0.10
Percentage male (10 points)	1.09 (0.92–1.30)	0.32	0.01	1.02 (0.82–1.27)	0.85	0.02	1.00 (0.81–1.23)	0.99
Percentage male leadership (10 points)	1.03 (0.93–1.13)	0.62	0.00	1.00 (0.89–1.13)	0.97	0.00	1.02 (0.91–1.14)	0.78
Postal code								
Average age (years)	0.89 (0.83–0.95)	0.00	0.07	0.96 (0.90–1.03)	0.26	0.02	0.93 (0.86–1.01)	0.08
Percentage male (10 points)	1.02 (0.76–1.37)	0.90	0.00	0.74 (0.57–0.95)	0.02	0.12	0.81 (0.60–1.08)	0.15

Table 4.8—Continued

Risk Factor	Bivariate			Adjusted for Prior Tiers			Adjusted, Including Current Tier	
	Risk Ratio (95% CI)	p-value	Tjur's D	Risk Ratio (95% CI)	p-value	Δ Tjur's D	Risk Ratio (95% CI)	p-value
Number of personnel (per 10,000)	0.93 (0.79–1.09)	0.37	0.01	0.89 (0.76–1.05)	0.17	0.02	0.89 (0.74–1.06)	0.18
Percentage male leadership (10 points)	1.35 (0.93–1.97)	0.12	0.03	1.40 (1.00–1.95)	0.05	–0.03	1.24 (0.90–1.70)	0.19
Major command code (or monitored command code for the Marine Corps)								
Number of personnel (per 10,000)	1.01 (0.99–1.03)	0.35	0.01	1.01 (0.99–1.03)	0.27	0.02	1.01 (0.98–1.03)	0.64
Average age (years)	0.87 (0.83–0.92)	0.00	0.11	0.92 (0.86–0.98)	0.01	0.09	0.91 (0.84–0.99)	0.02
Percentage male (10 points)	1.26 (0.96–1.67)	0.10	0.02	0.92 (0.67–1.26)	0.59	0.00	0.82 (0.56–1.20)	0.30
Percentage male leadership (10 points)	1.45 (0.83–2.54)	0.20	0.02	1.16 (0.80–1.68)	0.44	–0.01	0.97 (0.65–1.43)	0.87
Separation from the military								
Separated from military	3.41 (1.58–7.36)	0.00	0.08	4.88 (2.27–10.49)	0.00	0.28	4.88 (2.27–10.49)	0.00

NOTE: We scaled Tjur's D by a factor of 100 to put it on a percentage-point scale.

Summary

Results from our analyses indicated that service women who were older and who were Asian or black had significantly lower risk of sexual assault. However, age accounted for a greater proportion of the difference in risk between assaulted and nonassaulted service women than race did. Together, these birth demographics accounted for 1.52 percentage points of the difference in risk between these two groups. When considering characteristics at entry, service women who reported having experiences consistent with sexual assault prior to joining the military demonstrated a substantially elevated risk of sexual assault. In addition, higher AFQT scores, serving in a branch other than the Air Force, and entry as an enlisted member rather than an officer were all associated with higher sexual assault risk. As a group, characteristics at entry improved the difference in risk between assaulted and nonassaulted service women by 4.33 percentage points beyond that accounted for by birth demographics, which made it the tier of factors that most contributed to predicting women's sexual assault, by a substantial margin. See Table 4.9 for each tier's Tjur's D and change in Tjur's D values, for both women and men, when predicting sexual assault.

Personal history characteristics of service women—namely, being single, having fewer dependents, and having never attended college—were also associated with increased risk of sexual assault. In addition, risk for women appeared to be significantly higher in some occupational groups, with the lowest rates found for those in the health care fields. Personal and career history factors minimally improved upon antecedent risk factors, improving the differentiation of risk between women who were and were not assaulted by only 0.85 percentage points. In analysis of Tier 4 (recent experiences), bivariate results showed that service women who were deployed, served overseas, or served on a ship in the past year were all more likely to have been sexually assaulted in the past year. However, after accounting for conceptually prior factors, serving overseas

Table 4.9
Tjur's D When Predicting Sexual Assault, by Model Tier

Tier	Women		Men	
	Tjur's D	Δ Tjur's D	Tjur's D	Δ Tjur's D
Tier 1: Birth demographics	1.52	1.52	0.20	0.20
Tier 2: Characteristics at the time of service entry	5.85	4.33	2.86	2.66
Tier 3: Personal and career history	6.70	0.85	3.27	0.41
Tier 4: Recent experiences	7.17	0.47	4.46	1.19

NOTE: We scaled Tjur's D by a factor of 100 to put it on a percentage-point scale. The model for a given tier includes all factors from earlier tiers. Δ Tjur's D indicates the improvement in Tjur's D from the simpler model used in the earlier tier.

was no longer a significant predictor of risk, and the effect of serving on a ship was attenuated. Among organizational characteristics, the percentage of the organization that was male appeared to be associated with elevated risk in some clusters. Results also showed that women who left the military recently had more than twice the risk of having had a past-year sexual assault than those who remained in the military. Like personal and career history characteristics, recent experiences did less to differentiate between assaulted and nonassaulted service women groups than Tiers 1 or 2 did, when controlling for those earlier factors.

Among service men, younger age, but not race, was significantly associated with sexual assault risk. As seen with service women, service men who reported experiences consistent with sexual assault prior to joining the military were at substantially elevated risk of having a past-year sexual assault. Serving in the Air Force was associated with lower risk than the other service branches, but, unlike for women, a higher AFQT score was not a significant risk factor.

For service men, being single and having fewer dependents were associated with increased risk of sexual assault. Among career history factors, only pay grade significantly improved upon the model, with members in the E4 pay grade again having the highest risk of assault. As seen with service women, when controlling for birth demographics and characteristics at entry, personal and career history factors provided only a small improvement in risk differentiation (0.41 percentage points) between assaulted and nonassaulted service men.

Serving overseas in the past year was the only recent history factor that significantly predicted risk when controlling for all antecedent risk factors, but it was not significant when also controlling for the conceptually similar risk factors of being deployed or being assigned to a ship. Men who left the military recently had almost five times the risk of having had a past-year sexual assault than those who remained in the military. The recent (past-year) experiences tier of factors modestly improved the differentiation of assaulted and nonassaulted service men, providing a 1.19–percentage point improvement over the model that included all previously considered factors. However, it appears that these recent experiences may be somewhat more important predictors of risk for men than for women.

Overall, characteristics at service entry provided the greatest improvement in model differentiation of assaulted and nonassaulted service members compared with the other tiers for both women and men. The second most important set of explanatory factors differed for women and men. For women, birth demographics accounted for the next-largest share of explained risk; for men, it was recent experiences. Indeed, men's age and race in Tier 1 explained less of their risk than any other tier of risk factors did.

CHAPTER FIVE

Risk Factors for Sexual Harassment

In the 2014 RMWS, sexual harassment in the past year affected approximately 21.6 percent of all service women and 7 percent of service men (Morral, Gore, and Schell, 2015a). Because it is far more common than sexual assault, the models of sexual harassment risk have much more information on which to establish associations. We estimated separate models for women and men and discuss their similarities and differences in this chapter. Because the model results are separated by gender, the models do not explicitly provide effects sizes for gender as a predictor of sexual harassment. However, the bivariate effect size is relatively large: The risk ratio of women relative to men is 3.26 (95% CI: 3.00–3.55; Tjur's D = 3.53 percentage points).

Sexual Harassment Risk Factors for Service Women

Paralleling our analyses of sexual assault risk factors, we first assess the association between birth demographic risk factors and past-year sexual harassment (Tier 1). We then consider characteristics at the time of service entry (Tier 2), personal and career history (Tier 3), and recent experiences (Tier 4).

Birth Demographics

We found that both Tier 1 birth demographic factors, age and race, were associated with past-year sexual harassment risk for service women (Table 5.1). With each additional decade of age, risk of sexual harassment declined by a factor of 0.70 meaning that a woman was only about 70 percent as likely to be sexually harassed as another who was ten years her junior. Additionally, compared with white women, Asian and black women faced lower risks of sexual harassment, whereas respondents in the Hispanic and other race categories faced higher risks.

The *adjusted, including current tier* model, which included both age and race, provides modest differentiation of those at highest and lowest risk of sexual harassment. For instance, if we knew nothing about service women's individual risk factors, we would be unable to distinguish between the risk of those who experienced sexual harassment in the past year and the risk of those who did not. We would assume

Table 5.1
Tier 1: Association Between Birth Demographics and Past-Year Sexual Harassment, Women

Risk Factor	Bivariate			Adjusted, Including Current Tier	
	Risk Ratio (95% CI)	p-value	Tjur's D	Adjusted Risk Ratio (95% CI)	p-value
Age (decades)	0.70 (0.67–0.73)	0.00	1.59	0.71 (0.69–0.74)	0.00
Race		0.00	0.72		0.00
Asian	0.78 (0.66–0.92)			0.81 (0.68–0.95)	
Black	0.74 (0.69–0.80)			0.76 (0.71–0.81)	
Hispanic	1.16 (1.07–1.26)			1.12 (1.03–1.21)	
Other	1.22 (1.08–1.37)			1.14 (1.01–1.28)	
White	1 (reference)			1 (reference)	

NOTE: We scaled Tjur's D by a factor of 100 to put it on a percentage-point scale. Because there are no earlier tiers, the bivariate and adjusted effect sizes are identical.

that both groups had the DoD average risk of approximately 21.6 percent. The predicted risk of sexual harassment from a model that included both age and race averaged approximately 23.3 percent for women who experienced sexual harassment in the past year and 21.1 percent for those who did not. This results in a Tjur's D of 2.15 percentage points for this model. (For a complete list of each tier's Tjur's D values for predicting sexual harassment, for both women and men, see Table 5.9 toward the end of this chapter.)

Characteristics at the Time of Service Entry

Table 5.2 provides the association between Tier 2 characteristics of service women and past-year sexual harassment (1) at the bivariate level, (2) when adding those characteristics to the model consisting of all Tier 1 factors (the *adjusted for prior tiers* columns), and (3) when controlling for all Tier 1 and Tier 2 factors (the *adjusted, including current tier* columns). As was the case with sexual assault of women, higher AFQT scores among enlisted personnel were associated with elevated risk of sexual harassment. For each additional 10 percentile points scored on the AFQT, women were exposed to 1.1 times greater risk of sexual harassment.

Active-duty women who reported experiencing a sexual assault prior to joining the military had more than twice the risk of having experienced a past-year sexual harassment. Moreover, this factor alone improved upon the Tier 1 model by a

Tjur's D of 2.69 percentage points, meaning that the ability of the model to differentiate the risk of sexual harassment among women who were and were not harassed was improved by 2.69 percentage points, a moderately large contribution to explaining risk in these groups.

Women's branch of service was an important predictor of harassment risk, having a Tjur's D's of more than 2 percentage points. In a model adjusting for Tier 1 birth demographics and all Tier 2 characteristics at entry, women in the Army, Navy, and Marine Corps faced comparable risks of sexual harassment; however, in each case, their risk was approximately twice that of women in the Air Force.

These strong Tier 2 factors led to a substantially improved prediction. Whereas, on average, active-duty women had a 21.6-percent risk of past-year sexual harassment, predicted risk from a model that included factors from Tiers 1 and 2 averaged 27.6 percent for women who experienced sexual harassment and 19.9 percent for those who did not. This corresponds to a Tjur's D of 7.73 percentage points, which is an improvement of 5.58 percentage points over the Tier 1 model.

Personal and Career History

Table 5.3 introduces the personal history and career history subgroups of Tier 3 risk factors. As before, the *adjusted for prior tiers* model controlled for all factors from the prior tier, and the *adjusted, including current tier* model additionally controlled for other factors from the same subgroup of factors.

Among the personal history factors, marital status and educational attainment both provided statistically significant improvements over the Tier 2 model, but the effects of these factors were relatively small. It appears that women who were single had a sexual harassment risk that was 1.12 times greater than those who were not single, and the only education level associated with a significant effect on risk was a graduate degree, which was associated with risk only 0.84 times as large as the risk for women with a high school diploma for both adjusted estimates. Each of these factors contributed a 0.06 or smaller percentage-point improvement to Tier 2 Tjur's D, meaning that they uniquely predicted only a small portion of the variation in sexual harassment risk across the military.

Several career history factors provided considerably more predictive power, though still far less than was seen for the characteristics at entry in Tier 2. Pay grade was a significant predictor for both adjusted estimates: E4 service members had significantly greater risk than all other pay grades other than the O1–O3 group. Interestingly, the risk of sexual harassment for women in the E4 pay grade was significantly higher than that even of the E1–E3 pay grade group. However, neither a woman's promotion speed nor past deployments (between 2001 and 2013) improved the prediction of sexual harassment risk over the Tier 2 model.

Among Tier 3 factors, occupation group provided the greatest improvement in prediction of risk over the Tier 2 model. For enlisted members, occupation categories

Table 5.2
Tier 2: Association Between Characteristics at Entry and Past-Year Sexual Harassment, Women

Risk Factor	Bivariate			Adjusted for Prior Tiers			Adjusted, Including Current Tier	
	Risk Ratio (95% CI)	p-value	Tjur's D	Adjusted Risk Ratio (95% CI)	p-value	Δ Tjur's D	Adjusted Risk Ratio (95% CI)	p-value
AFQT score (10 points)[a]	1.14 (1.12–1.16)	0.00	1.23	1.12 (1.10–1.14)	0.00	1.00	1.10 (1.08–1.12)	0.00
Missing	0.59 (0.43–0.81)	0.00	0.04	0.76 (0.57–1.02)	0.07	0.01	1.01 (0.76–1.33)	0.96
Pre-service sexual assault	2.26 (2.11–2.41)	0.00	2.66	2.22 (2.09–2.36)	0.00	2.69	2.05 (1.92–2.18)	0.00
Service branch		0.00	2.29		0.00	2.05		0.00
Army	1.86 (1.74–1.98)			1.96 (1.83–2.09)			1.99 (1.87–2.13)	
Navy	2.24 (2.08–2.41)			2.11 (1.96–2.27)			2.03 (1.89–2.18)	
Air Force	1 (reference)			1 (reference)			1 (reference)	
Marine Corps	2.20 (1.98–2.44)			1.90 (1.70–2.11)			1.90 (1.71–2.11)	
Entry type		0.00	0.48		0.00	0.13		0.00
Enlisted[b]	1 (reference)			1 (reference)			1 (reference)	
Officer, academy	0.92 (0.81–1.05)			0.94 (0.82–1.07)			1.02 (0.89–1.16)	
Officer, ROTC	0.79 (0.72–0.87)			0.88 (0.80–0.96)			0.90 (0.82–0.99)	

Table 5.2—Continued

Risk Factor	Bivariate			Adjusted for Prior Tiers			Adjusted, Including Current Tier	
	Risk Ratio (95% CI)	p-value	Tjur's D	Adjusted Risk Ratio (95% CI)	p-value	Δ Tjur's D	Adjusted Risk Ratio (95% CI)	p-value
Officer, other	0.53 (0.48–0.59)			0.69 (0.62–0.77)			0.68 (0.61–0.75)	

NOTE: We scaled Tjur's D by a factor of 100 to put it on a percentage-point scale.

[a] AFQT scores are for enlisted members only.

[b] Enlisted includes warrant officers and those who went through Officer Candidate School.

Table 5.3
Tier 3: Association Between Personal and Career History and Past-Year Sexual Harassment, Women

Risk Factor	Bivariate			Adjusted for Prior Tiers			Adjusted, Including Current Tier	
	Risk Ratio (95% CI)	p-value	Tjur's D	Adjusted Risk Ratio (95% CI)	p-value	Δ Tjur's D	Adjusted Risk Ratio (95% CI)	p-value
Personal history								
Marital status (single)	1.30 (1.23–1.38)	0.00	0.46	1.11 (1.05–1.17)	0.00	0.06	1.12 (1.05–1.18)	0.00
Number of dependents	0.88 (0.86–0.90)	0.00	0.51	0.99 (0.96–1.01)	0.26	0.00	1.01 (0.98–1.03)	0.58
Educational attainment		0.00	1.02		0.03	0.03		0.03
Up to high school diploma	1 (reference)			1 (reference)			1 (reference)	
Some college	0.72 (0.67–0.78)			0.94 (0.87–1.02)			0.95 (0.88–1.02)	
Bachelor's degree	0.83 (0.77–0.89)			0.99 (0.90–1.08)			0.98 (0.90–1.07)	
Graduate degree	0.49 (0.45–0.54)			0.84 (0.74–0.96)			0.84 (0.74–0.96)	
Missing	0.93 (0.80–1.09)			1.04 (0.88–1.24)			1.03 (0.87–1.23)	
Career history								
Pay grade		0.00	1.85		0.00	0.37		0.00
E1–E3	0.82 (0.75–0.90)			0.79 (0.73–0.86)			0.84 (0.77–0.91)	
E4	1 (reference)			1 (reference)			1 (reference)	

Table 5.3—Continued

Risk Factor	Bivariate			Adjusted for Prior Tiers			Adjusted, Including Current Tier	
	Risk Ratio (95% CI)	p-value	Tjur's D	Adjusted Risk Ratio (95% CI)	p-value	Δ Tjur's D	Adjusted Risk Ratio (95% CI)	p-value
E5–E6	0.69 (0.64–0.74)			0.87 (0.81–0.94)			0.89 (0.82–0.96)	
E7–E9	0.43 (0.39–0.48)			0.67 (0.59–0.77)			0.69 (0.60–0.80)	
O1–O3	0.68 (0.63–0.74)			0.94 (0.81–1.09)			1.00 (0.82–1.23)	
O4–O6	0.33 (0.29–0.37)			0.61 (0.50–0.75)			0.66 (0.52–0.86)	
W1–W5	0.52 (0.40–0.68)			0.67 (0.51–0.88)			0.70 (0.50–0.96)	
Promotion speed (years)	1.03 (1.02–1.04)	0.00	0.16	0.99 (0.98–1.00)	0.22	0.01	1.00 (0.99–1.01)	0.83
Past deployment (years)	0.88 (0.85–0.92)	0.00	0.20	1.00 (0.97–1.04)	0.94	0.00	0.99 (0.96–1.03)	0.80
Occupation group (enlisted)		0.00	2.07		0.00	0.80		0.00
Infantry, gun crews, and seamanship specialists	0.69 (0.56–0.85)			0.85 (0.71–1.02)			0.88 (0.73–1.05)	
Electronic equipment repairers	1.05 (0.93–1.20)			0.97 (0.86–1.09)			0.95 (0.85–1.07)	
Communications and intelligence specialists	0.88 (0.78–0.99)			0.87 (0.77–0.97)			0.87 (0.77–0.98)	
Health care specialists	0.64 (0.57–0.71)			0.72 (0.65–0.80)			0.72 (0.65–0.81)	

Table 5.3—Continued

Risk Factor	Bivariate		Adjusted for Prior Tiers				Adjusted, Including Current Tier	
	Risk Ratio (95% CI)	p-value	Tjur's D	Adjusted Risk Ratio (95% CI)	p-value	Δ Tjur's D	Adjusted Risk Ratio (95% CI)	p-value
Other technical and allied specialists	0.73 (0.61–0.87)			0.80 (0.68–0.95)			0.81 (0.68–0.95)	
Functional support and administration	0.58 (0.53–0.65)			0.75 (0.67–0.83)			0.76 (0.68–0.85)	
Electrical/mechanical equipment repairers	1 (reference)			1 (reference)			1 (reference)	
Craftsworkers	0.98 (0.79–1.22)			1.04 (0.85–1.27)			1.04 (0.85–1.27)	
Service and supply handlers	0.80 (0.70–0.90)			1.01 (0.90–1.14)			1.01 (0.90–1.14)	
Nonoccupational	0.39 (0.26–0.58)			0.40 (0.27–0.59)			0.44 (0.30–0.66)	
Occupation group (officer)								
Tactical operations officers	1 (reference)			1 (reference)			1 (reference)	
Intelligence officers	0.82 (0.66–1.01)			0.85 (0.69–1.05)			0.87 (0.71–1.07)	
Engineering and maintenance officers	0.85 (0.71–1.03)			0.84 (0.69–1.02)			0.84 (0.70–1.02)	
Scientists and professionals	0.57 (0.45–0.72)			0.61 (0.48–0.79)			0.64 (0.50–0.82)	
Health care officers	0.46 (0.39–0.54)			0.52 (0.43–0.62)			0.53 (0.44–0.64)	

Table 5.3—Continued

Risk Factor	Bivariate			Adjusted for Prior Tiers			Adjusted, Including Current Tier	
	Risk Ratio (95% CI)	*p*-value	Tjur's D	Adjusted Risk Ratio (95% CI)	*p*-value	Δ Tjur's D	Adjusted Risk Ratio (95% CI)	*p*-value
Administrators	0.67 (0.55–0.81)			0.72 (0.59–0.87)			0.74 (0.61–0.90)	
Supply, procurement, and allied offices	0.69 (0.56–0.85)			0.72 (0.58–0.89)			0.73 (0.59–0.90)	
Other	1.16 (0.88–1.52)			0.97 (0.74–1.27)			0.95 (0.73–1.24)	

NOTE: We scaled Tjur's D by a factor of 100 to put it on a percentage-point scale.

with the lowest risk of sexual harassment included health care specialists, functional support and administration, and nonoccupational (which includes prisoners, students, trainees, and other roles not designated as an occupation). In contrast, women who were electrical/mechanical equipment repairers, service and supply handlers, or crafts-workers had a higher risk of sexual harassment.

For officers, the occupation with the highest sexual harassment risk was tactical operations. The groups with the lowest risk, and significantly lower than tactical operations, were scientists and professionals; health care providers; administrators; and those engaged in supply, procurement, and allied functions. These occupations were associated with lower risk by a factor of between 0.53 and 0.74, or risk that was roughly half to three-quarters that of tactical operations officers.

Together, the Tier 3 factors contributed modestly to the model combining all Tier 1 and Tier 2 factors. The predicted risk of sexual harassment from a model that included factors from Tiers 1–3 averaged approximately 28.6 percent for women who experienced sexual harassment in the prior year and 19.7 percent for those who did not. This corresponds to a Tjur's D of 8.90 percentage points, which is an improvement of 1.16 percentage points for this model relative to the model with Tier 1 and Tier 2 factors.

Recent Experiences

Tier 4 risk factors are categorized into three subgroups, each of which we evaluated separately using the *adjusted, including current tier* models (Table 5.4). Of the Tier 4 risk factors, being deployed and being assigned to a ship in the past 12 months each explained significantly more of the variance in past-year sexual harassment when controlling for factors included in Tiers 1 through 3. However, only serving on a ship was significant when controlling for deployment in the past 12 months and service overseas (OCONUS).

As noted earlier, we evaluated past-year organizational characteristics at three organizational levels: the service member's duty unit (based on unit identification code), installation (based on postal code), and major command (based on major command codes for the Army, Navy, and Air Force and monitored command codes for the Marine Corps). As seen in the *adjusted for prior tiers* column of Table 5.4, the average age of personnel, the percentage of the organization that was male, and the number of personnel in the organization significantly predicted risk for all three organizational levels. In contrast, having a higher or lower percentage of leadership that was male than the remainder of the organization was not a significant predictor at any level.

In the *adjusted, including current tier* estimates, which we ran separately for each of the three organizational levels, only percentage male was consistently a significant predictor across all levels. The effect sizes were quite similar, ranging from 1.07 to 1.10. Thus, as the percentage of men at each organizational unit increased by 10 percentage points, women's risk of sexual harassment increased by 7 percent to 10 per-

Table 5.4
Tier 4: Association Between Recent Experiences and Past-Year Sexual Harassment, Women

Risk Factor	Bivariate			Adjusted for Prior Tiers			Adjusted, Including Current Tier	
	Risk Ratio (95% CI)	p-value	Tjur's D	Risk Ratio (95% CI)	p-value	Δ Tjur's D	Risk Ratio (95% CI)	p-value
Recent history								
Deployed in the past 12 months	1.25 (1.11–1.40)	0.00	0.10	1.18 (1.06–1.31)	0.00	0.06	1.10 (0.99–1.22)	0.09
Location (OCONUS)	1.02 (0.95–1.10)	0.62	0.00	1.01 (0.95–1.08)	0.72	0.00	1.01 (0.94–1.08)	0.83
Assigned to a ship (past 12 months)	2.06 (1.85–2.29)	0.00	1.38	1.44 (1.28–1.62)	0.00	0.39	1.41 (1.25–1.58)	0.00
Past-year organizational characteristics								
Unit identification code								
Number of personnel (per 1,000)	1.28 (1.22–1.34)	0.00	1.11	1.12 (1.06–1.18)	0.00	0.24	1.11 (1.05–1.17)	0.00
Average age (years)	0.95 (0.94–0.95)	0.00	1.15	0.99 (0.98–1.00)	0.01	0.04	0.99 (0.99–1.00)	0.23
Percentage male (10 points)	1.18 (1.16–1.20)	0.00	1.03	1.08 (1.05–1.11)	0.00	0.13	1.09 (1.06–1.12)	0.00
Percentage male leadership (10 points)	1.04 (1.03–1.06)	0.00	0.11	1.01 (0.99–1.02)	0.42	0.00	1.02 (1.00–1.04)	0.04
Postal code								
Number of personnel (per 10,000)	1.06 (1.04–1.08)	0.00	0.15	1.03 (1.01–1.06)	0.01	0.03	1.01 (0.99–1.04)	0.33
Average age (years)	0.92 (0.91–0.93)	0.00	1.07	0.97 (0.96–0.98)	0.00	0.13	0.98 (0.96–0.99)	0.00

Table 5.4—Continued

Risk Factor	Bivariate			Adjusted for Prior Tiers				Adjusted, Including Current Tier	
	Risk Ratio (95% CI)	p-value	Tjur's D	Risk Ratio (95% CI)	p-value	Δ Tjur's D		Risk Ratio (95% CI)	p-value
Percentage male (10 points)	1.24 (1.19–1.31)	0.00	0.50	1.08 (1.03–1.14)	0.00	0.07		1.07 (1.01–1.14)	0.02
Percentage male leadership (10 points)	1.10 (1.04–1.16)	0.00	0.08	1.02 (0.97–1.07)	0.46	0.00		1.05 (0.99–1.11)	0.09
Major command code (or monitored command code for the Marine Corps)									
Number of personnel (per 10,000)	1.02 (1.01–1.02)	0.00	0.60	1.01 (1.01–1.02)	0.00	0.33		1.01 (1.01–1.02)	0.00
Average age (years)	0.91 (0.90–0.92)	0.00	1.39	0.98 (0.97–0.99)	0.00	0.06		1.01 (0.99–1.02)	0.31
Percentage male (10 points)	1.36 (1.30–1.42)	0.00	0.91	1.15 (1.09–1.22)	0.00	0.14		1.10 (1.03–1.18)	0.00
Percentage male leadership (10 points)	1.35 (1.25–1.46)	0.00	0.31	1.01 (0.94–1.08)	0.79	0.00		1.05 (0.97–1.15)	0.22
Separation from the military									
Separated from military	1.42 (1.05–1.91)	0.02	0.04	1.42 (1.08–1.87)	0.01	0.04		1.42 (1.08–1.87)	0.01

NOTE: We scaled Tjur's D by a factor of 100 to put it on a percentage-point scale.

cent. Other results were not fully consistent across the three levels of the organization, although it appears that risk was highest in environments with younger personnel or in larger units, installations, or commands. In any case, these organizational characteristics contributed a modest amount to the overall model of risk to women, as the largest improvement in Tjur's D across them all was 0.3 percentage points.

The last subgroup in Tier 4 contains the single factor indicating whether the service member separated from the military between when the RMWS sample was drawn and the end of the survey field period. This factor significantly improved upon models that included factors in Tiers 1–3: After controlling for all factors from prior tiers, including age, rank, and service, women who separated from the military had 1.42 times the risk of sexual harassment in the past year as those who remained.

The predicted risk of sexual harassment from a model that included factors from all tiers averaged approximately 29.4 percent for women who experienced sexual harassment in the past year and 19.4 percent for those who did not. This corresponds to a Tjur's D of 9.94 percentage points and represents an improvement in Tjur's D of 1.05 percentage points for this model over a model that included factors from Tiers 1–3.

Sexual Harassment Risk Factors for Service Men

We next consider the sexual harassment risk factors for service men. These analyses follow the same four-tier process that we used for service women.

Birth Demographics

Age and race were both significant birth demographic predictors of men's sexual harassment risk (Table 5.5). With each additional decade of age, the risk that men would be harassed declined by a factor of 0.66 in adjusted analyses. In addition, Hispanic men had 1.29 times the risk of past-year sexual harassment as white men. Combined, these factors helped differentiate the average modeled risk of service men who were and were not sexually harassed in the past year. On average, an estimated 6.6 percent of service men experienced sexual harassment in the year prior to the survey. The predicted risk of sexual harassment from a model that included only birth demographics averaged approximately 7.3 percent for men who experienced sexual harassment in the past year and 6.6 percent for those who did not. This represents a Tjur's D of 0.72 percentage points for this model.

Table 5.5
Tier 1: Association Between Birth Demographics and Past-Year Sexual Harassment, Men

Risk Factor	Bivariate			Adjusted, Including Current Tier	
	Risk Ratio (95% CI)	*p*-value	Tjur's D	Adjusted Risk Ratio (95% CI)	*p*-value
Age (decades)	0.65 (0.59–0.72)	0.00	0.59	0.66 (0.60–0.73)	0.00
Race		0.01	0.15		0.04
Asian	1.14 (0.77–1.67)			1.15 (0.78–1.69)	
Black	0.79 (0.62–1.01)			0.81 (0.63–1.03)	
Hispanic	1.33 (1.05–1.69)			1.29 (1.02–1.64)	
Other	1.29 (0.83–2.01)			1.20 (0.77–1.85)	
White	1 (reference)			1 (reference)	

NOTE: We scaled Tjur's D by a factor of 100 to put it on a percentage-point scale. Because there are no earlier tiers, the bivariate and adjusted effect sizes are identical.

Characteristics at the Time of Service Entry

Table 5.6 shows the estimated effect sizes of Tier 2 characteristics at entry for men. According to our analyses, AFQT scores had a positive association with risk: For every additional 10 percentage points on the test, risk of past-year sexual harassment increased by 10 percent. Experiencing sexual assault prior to joining the military was associated with more than five times the risk of experiencing sexual harassment in the past year, and this factor made a substantial contribution to explaining total population risk over models that included only the Tier 1 birth demographics. This contribution is illustrated by a change in Tjur's D of 1.25 percentage points, meaning that the ability of the model to differentiate the risk of sexual harassment among men who were and were not harassed was improved by an additional 1.25 percentage points. Branch of service was also a significant predictor of risk, as men in the Air Force had significantly lower risk than those in other services had. When controlling for all other Tier 1 and Tier 2 factors, Marines were 1.60 times more likely than airmen to report past-year sexual harassment, and Army soldiers and Navy sailors were, respectively, 2.44 and 2.40 times more likely than airmen to report. Finally, entry type had a significant association with risk: Men who entered service as officers had between 0.61 and 0.70 times the risk of enlistees.

The Tier 2 characteristics at entry made a large contribution to explaining service men's risk of past-year sexual harassment over and above Tier 1 birth demographics.

Table 5.6
Tier 2: Association Between Characteristics at Entry and Past-Year Sexual Harassment, Men

Risk Factor	Bivariate			Adjusted for Prior Tiers			Adjusted, Including Current Tier	
	Risk Ratio (95% CI)	p-value	Tjur's D	Adjusted Risk Ratio (95% CI)	p-value	Δ Tjur's D	Adjusted Risk Ratio (95% CI)	p-value
AFQT score (10 points)[a]	1.11 (1.05–1.17)	0.00	0.24	1.10 (1.05–1.17)	0.00	0.25	1.10 (1.04–1.15)	0.00
Missing	0.73 (0.39–1.39)	0.34	0.00	0.97 (0.54–1.75)	0.92	0.00	1.07 (0.61–1.86)	0.82
Pre-service sexual assault	5.46 (4.02–7.40)	0.00	1.13	5.39 (4.04–7.21)	0.00	1.25	5.08 (3.72–6.92)	0.00
Service branch		0.00	0.60		0.00	0.72		0.00
Army	2.33 (1.94–2.81)			2.41 (1.99–2.90)			2.44 (2.03–2.92)	
Navy	2.55 (2.05–3.17)			2.46 (1.98–3.05)			2.40 (1.93–2.97)	
Air Force	1 (reference)			1 (reference)			1 (reference)	
Marine Corps	1.86 (1.41–2.45)			1.56 (1.19–2.06)			1.60 (1.22–2.10)	
Entry type		0.00	0.22		0.00	0.08		0.00
Enlisted[b]	1 (reference)			1 (reference)			1 (reference)	
Officer, academy	0.56 (0.40–0.79)			0.64 (0.46–0.90)			0.70 (0.50–0.98)	
Officer, ROTC	0.48 (0.39–0.59)			0.59 (0.47–0.73)			0.61 (0.49–0.76)	

Table 5.6—Continued

Risk Factor	Bivariate			Adjusted for Prior Tiers			Adjusted, Including Current Tier	
	Risk Ratio (95% CI)	p-value	Tjur's D	Adjusted Risk Ratio (95% CI)	p-value	Δ Tjur's D	Adjusted Risk Ratio (95% CI)	p-value
Officer, other	0.48 (0.36–0.63)			0.68 (0.52–0.91)			0.65 (0.49–0.87)	

NOTE: We scaled Tjur's D by a factor of 100 to put it on a percentage-point scale.

a AFQT scores are for enlisted members only.

b Enlisted includes warrant officers and those who went through Officer Candidate School.

Whereas the average risk of sexual harassment was 6.6 percent across all active-duty men, predicted risk of sexual harassment from a model that included factors from Tiers 1 and 2 averaged approximately 9.4 percent for men who experienced sexual harassment in the past year and 6.4 percent for those who did not. This corresponds to a Tjur's D of 2.99 percentage points and represents an improvement in Tjur's D of 2.27 percentage points for this model relative to the Tier 1 model.

Personal and Career History

Tier 3 personal and career history factors are presented in Table 5.7. Although all of service men's personal history factors had a bivariate association with harassment risk, their effects sizes were substantially reduced when controlling for factors in Tiers 1 and 2.

Among career history factors, pay grade was significant in all models and explained a substantial portion of population risk over and above the factors in Tiers 1 and 2. Specifically, it accounted for a change in Tjur's D of 1.1 percentage point. As was the case for service women, men in the E4 pay grade had the highest risk of past-year sexual harassment after controlling for other career history factors and those in prior tiers. Indeed, E4 service members had almost twice the risk of enlisted members in the E5–E7 pay grades and approximately five times the risk of officers. Compared with E4 men, those in the E1–E3 pay grades had just 0.61 times the risk of sexual harassment.

Past deployments between 2001 and 2013 had a small but statistically significant association with risk: For every additional year of deployment, men faced 0.89 times as much risk of past-year sexual harassment. That is, after accounting for age and other factors, a year of deployment was associated with an 11-percent reduction in risk. Occupation group also had a significant overall association with risk, although the effect was small enough that no occupational categories among enlisted members had significantly higher or lower risk than electrical/mechanical equipment repairers, our reference group. Most occupation groups for officers were also not statistically different from the reference group of tactical operations; the only exception was that men in the "other" group faced more than twice the risk of men in tactical operations.

The predicted risk of sexual harassment from a model that included factors from Tiers 1, 2, and 3 averaged approximately 10.8 percent for men who experienced sexual harassment in the past year and 6.3 percent for those who did not. This corresponds to a Tjur's D of 4.48 percentage points and represents an improvement in Tjur's D of 1.50 percentage points over the model that included factors from Tiers 1 and 2.

Table 5.7
Tier 3: Association Between Personal and Career History and Past-Year Sexual Harassment, Men

Risk Factor	Bivariate			Adjusted for Prior Tiers			Adjusted, Including Current Tier	
	Risk Ratio (95% CI)	p-value	Tjur's D	Adjusted Risk Ratio (95% CI)	p-value	Δ Tjur's D	Adjusted Risk Ratio (95% CI)	p-value
Personal history								
Marital status (single)	1.45 (1.24–1.71)	0.00	0.25	1.13 (0.93–1.38)	0.21	0.02	1.04 (0.84–1.30)	0.70
Number of dependents	0.86 (0.82–0.90)	0.00	0.35	0.94 (0.89–1.00)	0.04	0.05	0.95 (0.89–1.01)	0.10
Educational attainment		0.00	0.31		0.98	0.00		0.97
Up to high school diploma	1 (reference)			1 (reference)			1 (reference)	
Some college	0.72 (0.56–0.93)			0.91 (0.68–1.22)			0.91 (0.68–1.22)	
Bachelor's degree	0.73 (0.60–0.89)			0.96 (0.75–1.24)			0.94 (0.73–1.22)	
Graduate degree	0.42 (0.34–0.51)			0.94 (0.70–1.27)			0.92 (0.68–1.24)	
Missing	0.73 (0.49–1.08)			0.94 (0.62–1.43)			0.92 (0.60–1.40)	
Career history								
Pay grade		0.00	1.74		0.00	1.07		0.00
E1–E3	0.59 (0.46–0.76)			0.62 (0.48–0.80)			0.61 (0.47–0.79)	
E4	1 (reference)			1 (reference)			1 (reference)	

Table 5.7—Continued

Risk Factor	Bivariate			Adjusted for Prior Tiers			Adjusted, Including Current Tier	
	Risk Ratio (95% CI)	p-value	Tjur's D	Adjusted Risk Ratio (95% CI)	p-value	Δ Tjur's D	Adjusted Risk Ratio (95% CI)	p-value
E5–E6	0.46 (0.38–0.54)			0.49 (0.40–0.59)			0.54 (0.43–0.67)	
E7–E9	0.20 (0.16–0.25)			0.22 (0.17–0.30)			0.26 (0.18–0.37)	
O1–O3	0.37 (0.30–0.46)			0.37 (0.27–0.51)			0.33 (0.22–0.49)	
O4–O6	0.17 (0.13–0.22)			0.18 (0.11–0.29)			0.18 (0.10–0.31)	
W1–W5	0.21 (0.13–0.32)			0.20 (0.12–0.33)			0.21 (0.12–0.37)	
Promotion speed (years)	1.01 (0.99–1.03)	0.21	0.01	0.96 (0.93–0.98)	0.00	0.08	0.98 (0.95–1.01)	0.18
Past deployment (years)	0.76 (0.70–0.83)	0.00	0.34	0.83 (0.76–0.90)	0.00	0.12	0.89 (0.81–0.98)	0.01
Occupation group (enlisted)		0.00	0.64		0.00	0.40		0.00
Infantry, gun crews, and seamanship specialists	1.05 (0.76–1.45)			0.86 (0.64–1.17)			0.89 (0.66–1.21)	
Electronic equipment repairers	1.20 (0.89–1.60)			1.06 (0.79–1.42)			1.06 (0.79–1.41)	
Communication and intelligence specialists	0.81 (0.60–1.10)			0.72 (0.54–0.97)			0.76 (0.56–1.01)	
Health care specialists	0.98 (0.73–1.32)			0.80 (0.59–1.08)			0.76 (0.57–1.02)	

Table 5.7—Continued

Risk Factor	Bivariate			Adjusted for Prior Tiers			Adjusted, Including Current Tier	
	Risk Ratio (95% CI)	p-value	Tjur's D	Adjusted Risk Ratio (95% CI)	p-value	Δ Tjur's D	Adjusted Risk Ratio (95% CI)	p-value
Other technical and allied specialists	0.86 (0.60–1.23)			0.86 (0.60–1.21)			0.83 (0.58–.18)	
Functional support and administration	0.74 (0.55–1.00)			0.76 (0.56–1.02)			0.78 (0.58–1.04)	
Electrical/mechanical equipment repairers	1 (reference)			1 (reference)			1 (reference)	
Craftsworkers	1.31 (0.85–2.02)			1.41 (0.93–2.14)			1.44 (0.96–2.17)	
Service and supply handlers	0.74 (0.55–0.98)			0.89 (0.67–1.17)			0.88 (0.67–1.15)	
Nonoccupational	0.46 (0.19–1.09)			0.45 (0.18–1.07)			0.54 (0.22–1.31)	
Occupation group (officer)								
Tactical operations officers	1 (reference)			1 (reference)			1 (reference)	
Intelligence officers	0.89 (0.56–1.42)			0.90 (0.56–1.44)			0.92 (0.57–1.47)	
Engineering and maintenance officers	0.87 (0.62–1.23)			0.93 (0.66–1.32)			0.90 (0.63–1.29)	
Scientists and professionals	0.94 (0.58–1.52)			1.11 (0.68–1.80)			1.13 (0.69–1.84)	
Health care officers	1.17 (0.83–1.64)			1.39 (0.91–2.12)			1.42 (0.94–2.15)	

Table 5.7—Continued

Risk Factor	Bivariate			Adjusted for Prior Tiers			Adjusted, Including Current Tier	
	Risk Ratio (95% CI)	p-value	Tjur's D	Adjusted Risk Ratio (95% CI)	p-value	Δ Tjur's D	Adjusted Risk Ratio (95% CI)	p-value
Administrators	0.90 (0.57–1.42)			0.97 (0.61–1.55)			0.92 (0.57–1.47)	
Supply, procurement, and allied officers	0.62 (0.37–1.04)			0.65 (0.38–1.11)			0.63 (0.37–1.07)	
Other	2.40 (1.43–4.04)			2.15 (1.29–3.59)			2.17 (1.31–3.60)	

NOTE: We scaled Tjur's D by a factor of 100 to put it on a percentage-point scale.

Recent Experiences

Table 5.8 shows the associations between recent experience risk factors (Tier 4) and past-year sexual harassment. Of the three highly correlated factors in the recent history subgroup, only being assigned to a ship in the past 12 months significantly predicted risk when controlling for factors in Tiers 1, 2, and 3. This factor remained a significant predictor in the *adjusted, including current tier* model, which controlled for location (OCONUS) and past-year deployment. Specifically, men with recent shipboard experience had 1.66 times the risk of past-year sexual harassment as those who were not assigned to a ship in the past year.

Characteristics describing the units, installations, and commands in which service men served in the past year were considered separately. In each set of analyses, the percentage of the organization's leadership that was male had no significant relationship to the risk of sexual harassment. In contrast, the average age of members in an organization, the overall percentage of them who were male, and the number of personnel in the organization were significant in most of the clusters when controlling for factors from earlier model tiers.

The lone risk factor in the final Tier 4 subgroup indicated whether men had separated from the military between the time the RMWS sample was drawn and the close of the survey field period. This factor was significant, indicating that men who separated from the military during this period were 2.28 times more likely to have been sexually harassed in the past year than those who did not separate, after controlling for all of the Tier 1–3 factors.

Men's predicted risk of sexual harassment from the final model that included factors from all tiers averaged approximately 11.6 percent for men who experienced sexual harassment in the past year and 6.3 percent for those who did not. This corresponds to a Tjur's D of 5.33 percentage points and represents an improvement in Tjur's D of 0.84 percentage points over the model that included factors from Tiers 1, 2, and 3.

Table 5.8
Tier 4: Association Between Recent Experiences and Past-Year Sexual Harassment, Men

Risk Factor	Bivariate			Adjusted for Prior Tiers			Adjusted, Including Current Tier	
	Risk Ratio (95% CI)	p-value	Tjur's D	Risk Ratio (95% CI)	p-value	Δ Tjur's D	Risk Ratio (95% CI)	p-value
Recent history								
Deployed in the past 12 months	1.12 (0.85–1.48)	0.42	0.01	1.03 (0.78–1.35)	0.83	0.00	0.99 (0.76–1.29)	0.96
Location (OCONUS)	1.24 (1.02–1.52)	0.03	0.06	1.16 (0.95–1.40)	0.14	0.05	1.13 (0.93–1.37)	0.22
Assigned to a ship (past 12 months)	2.30 (1.71–3.10)	0.00	0.47	1.69 (1.21–2.34)	0.00	0.22	1.66 (1.20–2.31)	0.00
Past-year organizational characteristics								
Unit identification code								
Number of personnel (per 1,000)	1.19 (1.02–1.38)	0.03	0.09	1.06 (0.90–1.25)	0.46	0.02	1.04 (0.88–1.23)	0.62
Average age (years)	0.93 (0.91–0.95)	0.00	0.46	0.97 (0.95–1.00)	0.03	0.07	0.98 (0.96–1.00)	0.06
Percentage male (10 points)	1.13 (1.05–1.22)	0.00	0.12	1.06 (0.98–1.15)	0.16	0.04	1.06 (0.98–1.15)	0.14
Percentage male leadership (10 points)	1.00 (0.96–1.05)	0.92	0.00	1.01 (0.96–1.06)	0.80	0.00	1.03 (0.97–1.08)	0.34
Postal code								
Number of personnel (per 10,000)	1.06 (1.03–1.09)	0.00	0.07	1.04 (1.00–1.08)	0.04	0.03	1.02 (0.97–1.07)	0.46
Average age (years)	0.90 (0.88–0.94)	0.00	0.38	0.93 (0.89–0.96)	0.00	0.26	0.94 (0.90–0.98)	0.00

Table 5.8—Continued

Risk Factor	Bivariate			Adjusted for Prior Tiers			Adjusted, Including Current Tier	
	Risk Ratio (95% CI)	p-value	Tjur's D	Risk Ratio (95% CI)	p-value	Δ Tjur's D	Risk Ratio (95% CI)	p-value
Percentage male (10 points)	1.33 (1.17–1.52)	0.00	0.18	1.20 (1.04–1.38)	0.01	0.10	1.12 (0.95–1.32)	0.17
Percentage male leadership (10 points)	0.96 (0.81–1.13)	0.60	0.00	0.96 (0.82–1.13)	0.64	0.01	1.03 (0.86–1.24)	0.73
Major command code (or monitored command code for the Marine Corps)								
Number of personnel (per 10,000)	1.03 (1.02–1.03)	0.00	0.36	1.02 (1.01–1.03)	0.00	0.16	1.01 (1.00–1.02)	0.04
Average age (years)	0.91 (0.89–0.93)	0.00	0.39	0.93 (0.90–0.96)	0.00	0.18	0.95 (0.92–0.99)	0.01
Percentage male (10 points)	1.23 (1.10–1.38)	0.00	0.11	1.16 (1.00–1.33)	0.04	0.04	1.10 (0.93–1.31)	0.25
Percentage male leadership (10 points)	1.30 (1.03–1.65)	0.03	0.06	1.07 (0.88–1.29)	0.50	0.01	1.05 (0.83–1.32)	0.70
Separation from the military								
Separated from military	1.92 (1.12–3.31)	0.02	0.09	2.28 (1.36–3.80)	0.00	0.16	2.28 (1.36–3.80)	0.00

NOTE: We scaled Tjur's D by a factor of 100 to put it on a percentage-point scale.

Summary

When examining birth demographic risk factors for sexual harassment among service women, being older in age and being Asian or black were significantly associated with lower risk, and age and race differentiated the risk of service women who had been sexually harassed in the past year and the risk of those who had not by 2.15 percentage points. Including characteristics at entry in the model (Tier 2) identified several additional predictors. Higher AFQT scores among enlisted women were associated with elevated risk of sexual harassment. Furthermore, women classified as having experienced a sexual assault prior to joining the military had a much higher risk of past-year sexual harassment. Branch of service was also a strong predictor of harassment risk, with women in the Air Force exposed to significantly lower risk than those in other services were. Characteristics at entry improved the risk differentiation between harassed and nonharassed service women by 5.58 percentage points over the Tier 1 model. See Table 5.9 for each tier's Tjur's D and change in Tjur's D values, for both women and men, when predicting sexual harassment.

Among personal and career history factors (Tier 3), being single and having lower educational attainment both elevated risk of sexual harassment, but these effects were associated with only a small improvement in the model's ability to differentiate between higher- and lower-risk populations. Among career history factors, pay grade was a significant risk predictor, as E4 service members had significantly greater risk than all other pay grades other than the O1–O3 group. Occupation group provided the greatest improvement in prediction of risk over antecedent risk factors. Overall, personal and career history factors improved upon differentiation of harassed and nonharassed women by 1.16 percentage points over the model with factors from Tiers 1 and 2.

Among recent experiences, being assigned to a ship was significantly associated with increased risk of harassment. Considering the various past-year organizational characteristics, only percentage male was consistently a significant predictor of elevated risk across all three of the organizational levels we examined. In addition, women who separated from the military had higher risk of sexual harassment in the past year than those who remained in the military had. Recent experiences improved upon the differentiation of women who were and were not harassed by 1.05 percentage points over the model with Tier 1–3 factors.

Among men, being older and not being Hispanic reduced risk of sexual assault; however, in contrast with the role birth demographics played for service women, neither age nor race strongly differentiated harassed and nonharassed service men. Together, these factors accounted for only 0.72 percentage points of risk differentiation among men who were and were not harassed. When we added characteristics at entry (Tier 2) to the models, many of the observed associations were similar to those seen in analyses assessing harassment of service women. Just as with service women, AFQT scores had a positive association with risk of sexual harassment, sexual harassment prior to join-

Table 5.9
Tjur's D When Predicting Sexual Harassment, by Model Tier

Tier	Women		Men	
	Tjur's D	Δ Tjur's D	Tjur's D	Δ Tjur's D
Tier 1: Birth demographics	2.15	2.15	0.72	0.72
Tier 2: Characteristics at the time of service entry	7.73	5.58	2.99	2.27
Tier 3: Personal and career history	8.90	1.16	4.48	1.50
Tier 4: Recent experiences	9.94	1.05	5.33	0.84

NOTE: We scaled Tjur's D by a factor of 100 to put it on a percentage-point scale. The model for a given tier includes all factors from earlier tiers. Δ Tjur's D indicates the improvement in Tjur's D from the simpler model used in the earlier tier.

ing the military was associated with a higher risk of sexual harassment, and rates of harassment were lowest for the Air Force. Entry type had a significant association with risk of sexual harassment for men: Those who entered service as officers had between 0.61 and 0.70 times the risk of those who entered as enlisted. Overall, characteristics at entry improved upon differentiation of risk among harassed and nonharassed men by an additional 2.27 percentage points relative to a model that included only birth demographics.

Looking at personal and career history factors (Tier 3), none of the personal history factors was strongly associated with harassment when controlling for Tier 1 and Tier 2 factors. However, pay grade was a significant predictor in all models and explained a substantial portion of population risk. Men in the E4 pay grade had the highest risk of past-year sexual harassment. Past deployment (2001–2013) had a small but statistically significant association with risk, and occupation group also had a significant overall association. Personal and career history factors improved risk differentiation between harassed and nonharassed service men by 1.50 percentage points over a model that included only birth demographics and characteristics at entry. When we incorporated recent experiences (Tier 4) into the analysis, we found that being assigned to a ship in the past 12 months significantly predicted sexual harassment risk. The average age of an organization's members, the overall percentage of them who were men, and the number of personnel in the organization were associated with significantly elevated risk in all or two out of the three organizational levels (unit, installation, and major command) when controlling for factors from earlier tiers. When controlling for factors from Tiers 1–3, men who separated from the military were 2.28 times more likely to have been sexually harassed in the past year than those who did not separate were.

As was the case with prediction of sexual assault risk, characteristics at entry proved to be the strongest contributors to predicting sexual harassment risk among women and men. Similarly, for women, the birth demographics factors accounted for the second-largest share of explained risk of sexual assault and sexual harassment. For men, recent experiences were the second-strongest predictors of men's sexual assault risk, and personal and career history factors were the second-strongest predictors of sexual harassment risk.

CHAPTER SIX

Conclusions and Recommendations

The search for risk factors associated with sexual assault and sexual harassment has identified many plausible risk factors in military and other populations. Often, this research has examined a small number of potential risk factors, addressed self-reported risk factors, or involved analyses that exclude important known risk factors. In each case, the resulting associations could provide a misleading picture of the factors that are most important for understanding sexual assault and sexual harassment risk. The study for current report used a large and representative sample of the active-duty military to systematically assess many candidate risk factors whose effects were estimated in a conceptually guided series of models. This approach helps distinguish between correlations that appear to be unique to specific risk factors and those that are explained by theoretically preexisting factors. For instance, earlier research suggested that deployment is a sexual assault and harassment risk factor (LeardMann et al., 2013). We, too, found a strong association between deployment and both past-year sexual assault and past-year sexual harassment for women and men. However, when controlling for other associated but conceptually prior factors, such as age, the effect of deployment was reduced. Similarly, the large bivariate effect of pay grade was substantially reduced when controlling for birth demographics and characteristics at entry. At the same time, because this research relied on administrative and survey data, it did not assess and cannot comment on the relative contribution of other risk factors, such as alcohol use, risk perception, dating and sexual behavior, and organizational context (Classen, Palesh, and Aggarwal, 2005; Fitzgerald et al., 1997; Gidycz, McNamara, and Edwards, 2006; Ullman, 2003).

A Common Set of Risk Factors Is Associated with Sexual Assault and Sexual Harassment, for Both Women and Men

One of the striking findings across the four different sets of models we estimated (models of sexual assault and sexual harassment for men and women separately) was the high degree of similarity in the predictors across genders and across sexual assault and sexual harassment outcomes. One way to quantify the similarity in the pattern of effect sizes is to look at the correlation between the model coefficients across these different models. The model coefficients when predicting sexual assault were strongly correlated (r = 0.77) with the analogous coefficients predicting sexual harassment across both women and men. Similarly, the model coefficients for women were strongly correlated (r = 0.71) with the analogous coefficients for men, across both assault and harassment. Given this high degree of similarity in the effects across models, it is probably useful to think about a common set of risk factors for both women and men, and both sexual assault and sexual harassment.

To facilitate combining effects across models, we selected the factors across all tiers that were important for at least one of the four sets of models; these predictors are shown in Table 6.1. Specifically, the table includes all risk factors that ever resulted in an improvement in Tjur's D of at least 0.20 percentage points over a model that included all covariates from the earlier tiers. For each factor, we present the adjusted risk ratios that describe the pattern of effects for each factor across each set of risk estimates, the average improvement in Tjur's D across the four adjusted models (Δ Tjur's D), and an importance ranking based on those averaged effect sizes. The risk factors are listed in order of average importance. Not shown in the table is the strong association of gender with sexual assault and sexual harassment. With an average change in Tjur's D of 2.41, gender was nearly as good a predictor of service-wide risk as the strongest predictor among all the risk factors we evaluated, which was pre-service sexual assault (average change in Tjur's D was 2.48).

The table compares the effects for a given risk factor across the four models. Although there was considerable similarity in the effect sizes, there were also a few notable differences across the models. Experiencing pre-service sexual assault, being younger, and being single all showed more-extreme risk ratios with sexual assault than with sexual harassment. However, the Tjur's D effect sizes showed less of a difference across these two outcomes because of the higher prevalence of sexual harassment. Race was one of the few factors whose effects changed direction across women and men. White men were generally at lower risk than men in other racial groups for sexual assault and harassment; however, white women were generally at higher risk than women in other racial groups.[1]

Many elements of the sexual assault risk models described in this report are consistent with previous research. As reported by other researchers (Kilpatrick et al., 1997; Kimerling et al., 2007; LeardMann et al., 2013; Street, Rosellini, et al., 2016; Street, Stafford, et al., 2008), for both women and men, younger age and a marital status of single increased risk of sexual assault. Previous research on race-related risk has been inconsistent (Breiding et al., 2014; DMDC, 2013a; Kessler, 2014; Kilpatrick et al.,

---

[1]   The effect of race on sexual assault for men was not statistically significant. However, this nonsignificant effect was descriptively consistent with the significant effect of race on sexual harassment for men. An interaction between race and gender was also significant in predicting both sexual assault and sexual harassment. This suggests that the nature of the association was different for men and women.

Table 6.1
Comparison of the Important Predictors of Sexual Assault or Sexual Harassment

| Tier | Risk Factor | Sexual Assault | | Sexual Harassment | | Average Δ Tjur's D | Average Importance |
		Adjusted Risk Ratio, Women	Adjusted Risk Ratio, Men	Adjusted Risk Ratio, Women	Adjusted Risk Ratio, Men		
2	Pre-service sexual assault	4.40	17.95	2.22	5.39	2.48	1
1	Age (decades)	0.42	0.57	0.70	0.65	0.92	2
2	Service branch					0.86	3
	Army	1.73	3.29	1.96	2.41		
	Navy	2.03	4.93	2.11	2.46		
	Air Force	1 (reference)	1 (reference)	1 (reference)	1 (reference)		
	Marine Corps	2.08	3.26	1.90	1.56		
3	Occupation group					0.46	4
	Enlisted						
	Infantry, gun crews, and seamanship specialists	1.04	1.06	0.85	0.86		
	Electronic equipment repairers	0.84	0.81	0.97	1.06		
	Communications and intelligence specialists	0.79	0.45	0.87	0.72		
	Health care specialists	0.73	0.78	0.72	0.80		
	Other technical and allied specialists	0.93	0.66	0.80	0.86		
	Functional support and administration	0.89	1.41	0.75	0.76		

Table 6.1—Continued

Tier	Risk Factor	Sexual Assault		Sexual Harassment		Average Δ Tjur's D	Average Importance
		Adjusted Risk Ratio, Women	Adjusted Risk Ratio, Men	Adjusted Risk Ratio, Women	Adjusted Risk Ratio, Men		
	Electrical/mechanical repairers	1 (reference)	1 (reference)	1 (reference)	1 (reference)		
	Craftsworkers	1.20	0.54	1.04	1.41		
	Service and supply handlers	1.06	1.44	1.01	0.89		
	Nonoccupational	0.54	0.21	0.40	0.45		
	Officer						
	Tactical operations officers	1 (reference)	1 (reference)	1 (reference)	1 (reference)		
	Intelligence officers	1.07	1.04	0.85	0.90		
	Engineering and maintenance officers	0.87	0.78	0.84	0.93		
	Scientists and professionals	0.87	1.09	0.61	1.11		
	Health care officers	0.44	0.70	0.52	1.39		
	Administrators	0.90	1.15	0.72	0.97		
	Supply, procurement, and allied officers	0.76	1.16	0.72	0.65		
	Other	0.83	0.21	0.97	2.15		
2	AFQT score (10 points)	1.18	1.15	1.12	1.10	0.44	5

Table 6.1—Continued

Tier	Risk Factor	Sexual Assault		Sexual Harassment		Average Δ Tjur's D	Average Importance
		Adjusted Risk Ratio, Women	Adjusted Risk Ratio, Men	Adjusted Risk Ratio, Women	Adjusted Risk Ratio, Men		
3	Pay grade					0.43	6
	E1–E3	1.07	0.87	0.79	0.62		
	E4	1 (ref)	1 (ref)	1 (ref)	1 (ref)		
	E5–E6	0.80	0.62	0.87	0.49		
	E7–E9	0.64	0.27	0.67	0.22		
	O1–O3	1.04	0.31	0.94	0.37		
	O4–O6	0.77	0.32	0.61	0.18		
	W1–W5	1.04	0.17	0.67	0.20		
1	Race					0.27	7
	Asian	0.54	1.07	0.78	1.14		
	Black	0.71	1.64	0.74	0.79		
	Hispanic	0.87	1.29	1.16	1.33		
	Other	1.24	1.81	1.22	1.29		
	White	1 (reference)	1 (reference)	1 (reference)	1 (reference)		
4	Assigned to a ship (past 12 months)	1.45	1.85	1.44	1.69	0.20	8
4	Number of personnel in the major or monitored command code (per 10,000)	1.02	1.01	1.01	1.02	0.14	9
4	Separated from military	2.12	4.88	1.42	2.28	0.13	10

Table 6.1—Continued

| | | Sexual Assault | | Sexual Harassment | | | |
Tier	Risk Factor	Adjusted Risk Ratio, Women	Adjusted Risk Ratio, Men	Adjusted Risk Ratio, Women	Adjusted Risk Ratio, Men	Average Δ Tjur's D	Average Importance
4	Postal code average age (years)	0.97	0.96	0.97	0.93	0.12	11
3	Marital status (single)	1.63	1.50	1.11	1.13	0.08	14

NOTES: Adjusted risk ratios control for all factors from earlier tiers. CIs for these risk ratios, as well as detailed information of the covariates included in these estimates, can be found in Tables 4.1–4.8 and Tables 5.1–5.8. Average Δ Tjur's D is the average Δ Tjur's D over the four adjusted models. Importance is the rank of those average effect sizes among the 30 factors we investigated. Factors were classified as important if they resulted in an improvement in Tjur's D of at least 0.20 percentage points over a model that included all covariates from earlier tiers. This could occur in any of the four models. Gender could not be included as an effect in these models, but it is one of the best predictors of these outcomes, with an average bivariate Tjur's D of 2.41 percentage points, effectively tied with pre-service sexual assault as the risk factor that contributed most to predicting sexual assault and harassment among the factors that we investigated.

2007; Kimerling et al., 2007; LeardMann et al., 2013; Sadler et al., 2003; Street, Rosellini, et al., 2016). This may be related to our finding that racial effects varied across women and men and, to a lesser extent, across sexual assault and harassment outcomes. Our finding that having never attended college was associated with increased risk among service women was also consistent with other studies of military samples (Kessler, 2014; LeardMann et al., 2013; Sadler et al., 2003; Street, Rosellini, et al., 2016; for an exception, see Street, Stafford, et al., 2008). In both civilian (Classen, Palesh, and Aggarwal, 2005; Coxell et al., 1999; Elliott et al., 2004; Gidycz et al., 1993; Humphrey and White, 2000; Lalor and McElvaney, 2010; Littleton, Axsom, and Grills-Taquechel, 2009; Messman-Moore, Brown, and Koelsch, 2005; Roodman and Clum, 2001) and military samples (Kessler, 2014; LeardMann et al., 2013; Merrill et al., 1999; Sadler et al., 2003), prior sexual assault victimization has been one of the strongest predictors of future sexual assault. This was also true in our analyses for both women and men. For service women, but not men, the percentage of their organization that was male was associated with elevated sexual assault risk, which is consistent with other studies (Harned et al., 2002; Sadler et al., 2003). For occupation groups, unlike the Millennium Cohort Study team (LeardMann et al., 2013), we did not find that combat specialties (e.g., infantry, gun crews, and seamanship specialists) were associated with elevated risk. This may be due, in part, to slightly different classification of occupations between the current study and the Millennium Cohort Study. We did find that, among enlisted women, some occupations (communications and intelligence specialists, health care specialists, and electronic equipment repairers) were at lower risk of sexual assault than the reference occupation (electrical/mechanical equipment repairers), and like in the Millennium Cohort Study (LeardMann et al., 2013), female officers in health care occupations were at lower risk than the reference group (tactical operations). Finally, we replicated the finding that enlisted service members were at higher risk of sexual assault than officers were (LeardMann et al., 2013; Sadler et al., 2003; Street, Rosellini, et al., 2016) and that members of the Air Force were at lower risk than other services (LeardMann et al., 2013).

Results from the sexual harassment risk models were also consistent with prior research. Younger age, lower educational attainment, and a marital status of single all elevate risk of sexual harassment according to previous research with military samples (Harned et al., 2002; LeardMann et al., 2013; McDonald, 2012) and this study, although we found that the effects of marital status and educational attainment were relatively small. Unlike civilian samples, but consistent with military research (Buchanan, Settles, and Woods, 2008; DMDC, 2013b), white women were at higher risk of sexual harassment than Asian and black women, and Hispanic women were at higher risk than white women. In both civilian and military samples, the extent to which the workplace gender ratio is skewed toward men has been shown to increase the risk of sexual harassment in the environment. We replicated this finding for service women working in disproportionately male environments even after controlling for a wide range of other conceptually prior factors. For men, the percentage of the organization that was male was a significant predictor of sexual harassment against men at the installation and major command levels but not the unit level. After controlling for conceptually prior factors, we found that branch of service, entry type, and pay grade predicted sexual harassment risk for both service women and men, as has been true in other military studies (Buchanan, Settles, and Woods, 2008; DMDC, 2011, 2013b; Harned et al., 2002; LeardMann et al., 2013).

The role of AFQT scores is one finding from the current analysis that is notably different from prior research. Specifically, Kessler (2014) found that soldiers who had higher AFQT scores were less likely to file an unrestricted report of a sexual assault. The current study found that service members who had higher AFQT scores were more likely to experience a sexual assault in the past year. We hypothesized that findings in opposite directions may be attributable to the different measures of sexual assault. Service members with high AFQT scores may be more likely to experience an assault, but because they are substantially less likely to file an unrestricted report when they are assaulted, they appear to be at lower risk when analyzing reported assaults. To investigate this hypothesis, we looked at officially reported sexual assaults within the RMWS data. We found that, despite experiencing sexual assaults at a higher rate, individuals with high AFQT scores had lower rates of officially reported assaults. For instance, the average AFQT percentile score among enlisted members was higher among those who were sexually assaulted in the past year (68.9; 95% CI: 66.9–70.9) compared with those who were not (65.5; 95% CI: 65.3–65.8). However, those who filed an unrestricted report of sexual assault had a lower average AFQT score (62.6; 95% CI: 58.2–67.0) than those who were sexually assaulted but chose not to file a report (69.9; 95% CI: 67.7–72.0). This effect explains the different findings in the current research compared with those of Kessler (2014). It also raises questions about why this difference might occur. Possibly, the assaults on members with higher AFQT scores are systematically different in ways that make reporting a less attractive option. Alternatively, it may be that the assaults are similar, but those with higher AFQT scores perceive fewer benefits, or greater harms, from reporting relative to those with lower AFQT scores.

Risk of Sexual Assault and Risk of Sexual Harassment Are Strongly Associated with Separation from the Military

Across bivariate and adjusted models, separation from the military was strongly associated with risk of sexual assault and sexual harassment among women and men. Although the model was set up to treat separation as a predictor, it may be more useful to think about this association as resulting from the opposite temporal sequence, with sexual assault preceding, and increasing the likelihood of, separation from service. However, another possibility is that a third factor, not included in our analyses, is associated with both sexual assault risk and the likelihood of separating. Limited previous research suggests that sexual assaults in the military are associated with different aspects of separation, including separating with a service-connected disability and voluntarily separating earlier than intended (see, for example, Ghosh-Dastidar et al., 2015; Kimerling et al., 2007; Sadler et al., 2003). Additional research might consider potential third factors associated with (1) sexual assault and sexual harassment and (2) military separation. Future research might also further consider associations between different types of separation (e.g., voluntary or involuntary) and sexual assault and sexual harassment.

The Distribution of Sexual Assault Risk Across the Military

The final risk models for sexual assault and sexual harassment provide insights into many factors associated with risk, but they do not identify which specific individuals will be assaulted and which will not. Said another way, the predicted probabilities of sexual assault for most service members are far enough from either zero or one that there is still considerable uncertainty about which service members will experience an assault. For example, we would expect to observe about 1,900 past-year sexual assaults among the 10,000 men with the highest predicted risk and just two assaults among the 10,000 men with the lowest risk. For women, we would expect to observe about 2,400 assaults among the 10,000 women with the highest risk and 40 assaults among the 10,000 women with the lowest risk. Therefore, the models can predict large differences in observed numbers of sexual assaults for different groups, particularly when comparing the extremes of the risk distribution, even though they do not specify which individuals within each group will be assaulted.

It is likely that some of the remaining uncertainty about who will experience a sexual assault could be reduced if we had additional information about key risk factors. Although some of these omitted risk factors are likely to be characteristics that the literature has not yet identified as important, one of the best predictors of sexual assault risk in civilian samples, sexual orientation (see, for example, Black et al, 2011; Rothman, Exner, and Baughman, 2011), could not be included in the current analyses.[2] However, in the 2016 WGRA, sexual orientation and transgender status was assessed. Specifically, Davis, Vega, and McLeod (2017) reported that men who identified themselves as gay, bisexual, or transgender made up 3 percent of all active-duty service men and were exposed to more than ten times the risk of sexual assault as men who identified themselves as not gay, bisexual, or transgender (3.5 percent risk compared with

---

[2] Although RAND researchers proposed to assess sexual orientation in the 2014 RMWS, related questions and measures were removed because they were judged to violate DoD personnel policy at the time.

0.3 percent risk). This implies that more than one-fourth of all military men who were sexually assaulted in the past year were gay, bisexual, or transgender. Women who identified themselves as lesbian, bisexual, or transgender made up 12 percent of all active-duty women and faced almost twice the risk of sexual assault as other service women (6.3 percent risk compared with 3.5 percent risk). This implies that approximately one in five military women who were sexually assaulted in the past year were lesbian, bisexual, or transgender. Thus, it is likely that prediction of sexual assault in the military could be substantially improved by including sexual orientation in the models. In addition, knowing that sexual and gender minorities face elevated risks could be used to better understand the circumstances under which such assaults take place. Such an evaluation could help identify risk factors that military leaders could influence through control or prevention measures.

Another set of factors that might help explain individuals' risk of sexual assault and harassment is unit and installation climate and culture. It may be that there are variations across units in discipline, attitudes toward harassment, or accountability, for instance, that could help explain individuals' risk. The present study had no such climate and culture measures to include in our models of risk.

Recommendations

Our analyses suggest that several factors are associated with increased risk of sexual assault and sexual harassment among service women and men. DoD can use this information to modify programs and training that address sexual assault and sexual harassment. In this section, we describe recommendations that we drew from our results.

Use Risk Models to Inform Targeted Prevention and Response Activities

Those planning sexual assault and sexual harassment prevention efforts across the services can draw from the models in this report to inform their efforts. For example, prevention-relevant training could reference the identified risk factors to provide service members with more-accurate information on risk. In addition, commanders may draw from the information in these models to assess risk within their units, which could guide the frequency with which certain units receive prevention training and information. As seen in these models, risk of sexual assault and sexual harassment in the military is not equivalent across all service members and will vary across units, installations, commands, occupations, and other aggregations of service members. Models like those we developed here could be used to anticipate which such aggregations present the greatest risk to members and then to target training and prevention interventions.

DoD's *2014–2016 Sexual Assault Prevention Strategy* (DoD, 2014) highlights the potential utility of deterrence measures in preventing sexual assault. These include enhancements to physical security and surveillance, such as video cameras, patrols, and barracks monitors. However, such improvements are most likely to be effective if we can identify locations and individuals that are at high risk and target these prevention efforts toward them. Supervision could also be heightened via leadership training. Military leaders who identify and react to precursors of sexual harassment and sexual assault in these environments can send a top-down message that the environment is not a safe place to perpetrate. However, supervisors who are in areas of high risk of sexual assault and harassment need to know when their commands face especially heightened risk and ensure that leaders there give sexual assault prevention activities appropriate attention.

In practice, military planners who wish to use a risk model to guide policy may not have some of the predictors used in our models, which may restrict their ability to get an estimate of risk. For example, they will not have access to information on pre-service sexual assaults, which was the best single predictor. For this reason, in the appendix, we provide algorithms for calculating sexual assault and harassment risk for women and men using a simplified model of risk that uses only factors that are easily available in DMDC data.

Through Outreach and Victim Assistance, Support the Needs of Service Members Who Were Sexually Assaulted Prior to Joining the Military

Consistent with previous research (see Breitenbecher, 2001; Classen, Palesh, and Aggarwal, 2005; Messman-Moore and Long, 2000), we found that service women and men who experienced sexual assault prior to joining the military were at substantially elevated risk of sexual assault and sexual harassment in the military. Addressing the needs of service members who experienced sexual assault prior to joining the military may help prevent subsequent experiences of sexual assault or sexual harassment. DoD currently offers a tertiary prevention effort[3] in the form of a self-guided, online training for survivors of pre-service sexual assault or abuse, called "Building Hope and Resiliency: Addressing the Effects of Sexual Assault" (DoD, 2017). In addition, service members can access anonymous support through the DoD Safe Helpline, a website and telephone helpline that address service member sexual assault, including experiences that occurred prior to joining the military (DoD, undated). Similarly, DoD and service-specific resources, such as sexual assault response coordinators, advocacy services, and treatment for subsequent mental health conditions, are available to service members who have experienced sexual assault whether or not it occurred during military service.

To further address the needs of service members who experienced sexual assault prior to joining the military, DoD can modify current outreach to include additional material addressing those who have experienced pre-service assaults. This could include

---

[3] In sexual assault prevention, *tertiary prevention* refers to long-term efforts to prevent subsequent revictimization (Centers for Disease Control and Prevention, 2004).

clear and explicit statements about which services are available to pre-service sexual assault survivors. Without explicit reference to pre-service assaults, service members may misinterpret services as applying only to those who experienced sexual assaults after joining the military. This information should be placed in easily observable areas and on broad military service and installation-specific websites addressing sexual assault, including the DoD Safe Helpline homepage.

DoD might also consider using and evaluating tailored efforts for those who experienced pre-service assault that draw from promising previous research. For example, limited initial research suggests that cognitive behavioral interventions that identify and address risks and safety behaviors can help lower rates of violence revictimization (Ellsberg et al., 2015; Gilmore, Lewis, and George, 2015; Kiely et al., 2010; Yeater and O'Donohue, 1999). Notably, this research has focused on provision of services to women, so it is not clear what, if any, effects these would have for men.

Finally, we emphasize that we do not believe that it would be right or feasible to attempt to screen recruits for pre-service sexual assault experiences as a way to reduce the risk or frequency of assaults against service members. Barring admission to the military on the grounds of a prior sexual assault would further victimize such individuals and could be an illegal form of discrimination because of the differential impact across male and female recruits. Moreover, for most victims of sexual assault, the military would have to rely on applicants' self-reports of their history of victimization, because most sexual assaults are not reported to the police or other agencies. It seems likely that if a past sexual assault would disqualify an applicant, applicants would soon learn to withhold that information, possibly making it harder for them to access needed services once they join the military.

Conduct Research to Understand the Association Between Pre-Service and Recent Sexual Assault

Those who experienced pre-service sexual assault have substantially higher risks for sexual assault and sexual harassment in the military; of all the risk factors that we identified in this study, this one contributed most to the prediction of sexual assault, by a substantial margin. Yet, we do not understand exactly how to interpret this effect, which makes any recommendations about how to use this information to improve sexual assault prevention and response systems speculative. Specifically, it would be helpful for researchers to answer three broad questions:

1. *To what extent is the association caused by stable risk factors that were omitted from our models of risk?* That is, it could be that the association of risk with prior sexual assault is causally spurious. Instead, some other, unobserved characteristics of individuals might explain their elevated risk before and after entering the military. These unobserved risk factors could be victim characteristics (e.g., personality factors, alcohol consumption habits, sexual orientation, relationship

skills, physical appearance) or situational factors (e.g., continued contact with a previous perpetrator, living in a high-risk location). Each of these omitted risk factors would have somewhat different implications for sexual assault prevention and response. Research could address these alternative explanations by measuring a broader range of the proposed factors in studies, such as the WGRA, to better understand the origins of sexual assault risk and better develop prevention programs.

2. *To what extent does experiencing sexual assault cause the victim to be at increased risk of subsequent assault?* That is, it could be that prior sexual assault is a true risk factor, and may operate through several possible mechanisms. For example, the prior sexual assault may affect the victim's relationship expectations in a way that increases the chance for unhealthy and abusive relationships, or it may change the person's attitudes about sex in a way that makes subsequent unwanted sexual contact more likely. Investigating this may require longitudinal research that assesses these and other potential mechanisms of effect. If research can identify any such changes caused by an earlier assault, they may also serve as points of intervention where the association between prior sexual assault and future sexual assault could be broken.

3. *To what extent is the association between sexual assaults before and after joining the military a methodological artifact?* Although the association of prior sexual assault with future sexual assault is conceptually longitudinal, the actual research that has assessed this association has almost always been cross-sectional. Like in the current study, retrospective measures of both recent and earlier assaults are assessed at the same time and in the same research context. It is possible that a measure of pre-service sexual assault that was administered before entering service would be less associated with subsequent sexual assault than measures collected contemporaneously with military sexual assault measures. Investigating this possibility requires longitudinal research methods—for example, linking responses across multiple administrations of the WGRA or conducting additional data collection on early-career service members that can be linked to later WGRA data.

Investigate Why Risk Varies by Service Branch, Occupation Group, AFQT Score, and Other Characteristics

Some of the strongest predictors of sexual assault and sexual harassment risk that we identified are associated with aspects of military service. As a result, the risk reflected in these associations may be controllable by military leadership or policy. For instance, some occupations may have higher or lower risk because of working conditions that could be modified. Alternatively, some occupations may have higher risk for reasons that are less directly under the control of the services for reasons having to do with the types of people who gravitate toward those occupations or the unavoidable requirements of the jobs. Better information about why risk varies across service branches, occupations, AFQT scores, and other service-related risk factors could help the effort to craft targeted interventions to mitigate the risk. If, for instance, the reason service members with higher AFQT scores are more likely to be assaulted is because they are more likely to be ostracized or harassed, this would imply a much different prevention strategy than if the association of AFQT score and sexual assault risk is instead attributable to their greater ability to distinguish unwanted or abusive sexual contact from consensual contact. Therefore, risk-mitigation strategies would benefit from better information on the mechanisms by which these factors influence the risk of sexual assault and harassment.

This report demonstrates that risk of sexual assault and sexual harassment can be predicted sufficiently well to produce sharply different predicted rates of victimization, especially for women and men whose predicted risk is especially low or high. This differentiation is achieved using just characteristics of the service member, his or her job, and his or her work environment. Future models of risk could substantially improve upon those described here with the addition of known risk factors that were unavailable at the time this study was conducted (such as whether the member belongs to a sexual or gender minority) and with the inclusion of more-detailed information about service members' living and work environments (such as information on leadership climate and workplace hostility).

Simplified Risk Model

In this appendix, we provide algorithms for calculating sexual assault risk for women and men using a simplified model of risk that uses only risk factors that are easily available in DMDC data.

The starting point for the simplified model was a model that included all factors in Tiers 1 through 3, excluding pre-service sexual assault. In a reverse-stepwise procedure, we then pruned this model to progressively simpler models using an Akaike Information Criterion (AIC). At each stage, the next factor removed from the model was the one whose removal resulted in the best AIC. We simultaneously removed factors and their gender interaction and combined the AIC across both women and men. The final model represents the factor set with the best AIC—the most parsimonious model. All models were estimated using weighted data from active-duty RMWS respondents.

The set of risk factors included in the final reduced-risk model, along with their coefficients, are provided in Table A.1. We note the following details about the risk factors:

1. Age was measured in years.
2. Race was constructed from the Active Duty Master File variables called ETHNIC and HISPANIC.[1]
3. Education codes were derived from the first digit of the EDUCATION variable in the Active Duty Master File. All EDUCATION codes beginning with digits 1, 2, and 3 were combined into a single educational attainment category. Codes with initial digits of 4, 5, 6, and 9 were treated as four separate categories. Each category's description is shown in parentheses.

---

[1] The pseudocode for the constructed race factor is as follows:
If ETHNIC is any of ("AK", "AL", "AM", "AN", "AO"), then race = "Hispanic";
Otherwise:
1. if HISPANIC is any of ("005" or "999"), then race = "white";
2. else if HISPANIC = "003," then race = "black";
3. else if HISPANIC = "002," then race = "Asian";
4. else race = "other."

4. If AFQT score is missing, it was imputed as 66.1 for men and 62.4 for women.
5. Past deployment (2001–2013) measured the cumulative number of months a service member was deployed between September 2001 and July 2013 (before the survey was conducted). (In this appendix, we use months as the unit for this variable; in the main report, the unit of measurement was years.)
6. Occupation groups were derived from the first two or three digits of the DoD Occupation Group codes. Each category's description is shown in parentheses.

The expected sexual assault risk for collections of service members can be estimated from this reduced model. First, the risk of sexual assault for an individual service member can be estimated as

$$\text{Sexual assault risk} = \text{expit}(\beta_0 + \beta_1 * \text{Age} + \beta_2 * \text{Race} + \ldots + \beta_9 * \text{Occupation}),$$

where $\text{expit}(x) = e^x / (1 + e^x)$ is the inverse-logit function and $\beta_0 \ldots + \beta_9$ are the gender-specific coefficients in Table A.1.

The sexual assault risk for a collection of service members (e.g., a unit) is simply the average of the sexual assault risk of the service members in that group. For example, if there is a unit of 100 service members, we would first estimate the sexual assault risk for each of these 100 service members using the given equation and then average these 100 values to get the overall sexual assault risk for the unit.

This simplified model explains risk across service branches and genders well compared with the more complicated four-tier models described in the report. In particular, the four-tier model (excluding the pre-service sexual assault and separated from service risk factors, which are not available in administrative data for current service members) has a Tjur's D of 0.0326 combining both women and men. The reduced model described in this appendix has a Tjur's D of 0.0312, for a relatively small prediction loss (change in Tjur's D) of 0.0014.

Table A.1
Regression Coefficients for Simplified Sexual Assault Risk Models for Service Women and Men

	Women	Men
Intercept	−3.5187	−6.5216
Age (years)	−0.0420	−0.0008
Race		
Non-Hispanic white or missing race	0.0000	0.0000
Non-Hispanic Asian	−0.5663	−0.0847
Non-Hispanic black	−0.2338	0.4857
Hispanic	−0.2728	0.0876
Non-Hispanic other or mixed race	0.0058	0.2424
Service branch		
Army	0.6401	1.2954
Navy	0.5977	1.5707
Air Force	0.0000	0.0000
Marine Corps	0.7202	1.2306
Pay grade		
E1–E3	0.0583	−0.2162
E4	0.0000	0.0000
E5–E6	−0.1854	−0.2892
E7–E9	−0.4037	−1.1382
O1–O3	0.0796	−1.1327
O4–O6	−0.0774	−0.7230
W1–W5	−0.0003	−1.5196
Educational attainment		
1 through 3 (up to high school diploma)	0.0000	0.0000
4 (some college)	−0.2501	−0.2916
5 (bachelor's degree)	−0.3483	0.0499
6 (graduate degree)	−0.5835	−0.3944
9 (missing)	−0.0426	−0.1616

Table A.1—Continued

	Women	Men
Marital status (single)	0.5671	0.4007
AFQT score	0.0197	0.0144
Past deployment (2001–2013) (months)	−0.0021	−0.0132
Occupation group (enlisted)		
10 (infantry, gun crews, and seamanship specialists)	0.0932	0.0057
11 (electronic equipment repairers)	−0.2201	−0.2198
12 (communications and intelligence specialists)	−0.2313	−0.8851
13 (health care specialists)	−0.3177	−0.3907
14 (other technical and allied specialists)	−0.0709	−0.4275
15 (functional support and administration)	−0.1354	0.2646
16 (electrical/mechanical equipment repairers)	0.0000	0.0000
17 (craftsworkers)	0.1363	−0.6459
18 (service and supply handlers)	0.0369	0.2694
19 (nonoccupational)	−0.8030	−1.6233
Occupation group (officer)		
121 (general officers and executives)	−0.2311	−1.4208
122 (tactical operations officers)	0.0000	0.0000
123 (intelligence officers)	0.1809	0.1127
124 (engineering and maintenance officers)	−0.0812	−0.2536
125 (scientists and professionals)	0.1044	−0.1214
126 (health care officers)	−0.8666	−0.7758
127 (administrators)	−0.0067	0.1252
128 (supply, procurement, and allied officers)	−0.2493	0.2684
129 (nonoccupational)	−0.2311	−1.4208

NOTE: In the four-tier models described in the main report, we combined codes 121 and 129 into an "other" category.

References

Abbey, Antonia, Lisa Thomson Ross, Donna McDuffie, and Pam McAuslan, "Alcohol and Dating Risk Factors for Sexual Assault Among College Women," *Psychology of Women Quarterly*, Vol. 20, No. 1, 1996, pp. 147–169.

Adams-Curtis, Leah E., and Gordon B. Forbes, "College Women's Experiences of Sexual Coercion: A Review of Cultural, Perpetrator, Victim, and Situational Variables," *Trauma, Violence, and Abuse*, Vol. 5, No. 2, 2004, pp. 91–122.

Baron, R. M., and D. A. Kenny, "The Moderator–Mediator Variable Distinction in Social Psychological Research: Conceptual, Strategic, and Statistical Considerations," *Journal of Personality and Social Psychology*, Vol. 51, No. 6, 1986, pp. 1173–1182.

Berdahl, J. L, and C. Moore, "Workplace Harassment: Double Jeopardy for Minority Women," *Journal of Applied Psychology*, Vol. 91, No. 2, March 2006, pp. 426–436.

Bergman, M. E., and F. Drasgow, "Race as a Moderator in a Model of Sexual Harassment: An Empirical Test," *Journal of Occupational Health Psychology*, Vol. 8, No. 2, April 2003, pp. 131–145.

Black, M. C., K. C. Basile, M. J. Breiding, S.G. Smith, M. L. Walters, M. T. Merrick, J. Chen, and M. R. Stevens, *The National Intimate Partner and Sexual Violence Survey (NISVS): 2010 Summary Report*, Atlanta, Ga.: National Center for Injury Prevention and Control, Centers for Disease Control and Prevention, 2011.

Breitenbecher, Kimberly Hanson, "Sexual Revictimization Among Women: A Review of the Literature Focusing on Empirical Investigations," *Aggression and Violent Behavior*, Vol. 6, No. 4, 2001, pp. 415–432.

Breiding, Matthew J., Sharon G. Smith, Kathleen C. Basile, Mikel L. Walters, Jieru Chen, and Melissa T. Merrick, "Prevalence and Characteristics of Sexual Violence, Stalking, and Intimate Partner Violence Victimization: National Intimate Partner and Sexual Victimization Survey, United States, 2011," *Morbidity and Mortality Weekly Report*, Vol. 63, No. 35, September 5, 2014, pp. 1–18.

Buchanan, N. T., I. H. Settles, and K. C. Woods, "Comparing Sexual Harassment Subtypes Among Black and White Women by Military Rank: Double Jeopardy, the Jezebel, and the Cult of True Womanhood," *Psychology of Women Quarterly*, Vol. 32, No. 4, 2008, pp. 347–361.

Centers for Disease Control and Prevention, *Sexual Violence Prevention: Beginning the Dialogue*, Atlanta, Ga.: U.S. Department of Health and Human Services, 2004.

Champion, Heather L. O., Kristie Long Foley, Robert H. Durant, Rebecca Hensberry, David Altman, and Mark Wolfson, "Adolescent Sexual Victimization, Use of Alcohol and Other Substances, and Other Health Risk Behaviors," *Journal of Adolescent Health*, Vol. 35, No. 4, 2004, pp. 321–328.

Chu, H., and S. Cole, "Estimation of Risk Ratios in Cohort Studies with Common Outcomes: A Bayesian Approach," *Epidemiology*, Vol. 21, No. 6, 2010, pp. 855–862.

Classen, Catherine C., Oxana Gronskaya Palesh, and Rashi Aggarwal, "Sexual Revictimization: A Review of the Empirical Literature," *Trauma, Violence, and Abuse*, Vol. 6, No. 2, 2005, pp. 103–129.

Cohen, Jacob, Patricia Cohen, Steven G. West, and Leona S. Aiken, *Applied Multiple Regression/Correlation Analysis for the Behavioral Sciences*, 3rd ed., New York: Routledge, 2002.

Coxell, A. W., M. King, G. Mezey, and D. Gordon, "Lifetime Prevalence, Characteristics and Associated Problems of Non-Consensual Sex in Men: Cross Sectional Survey," *BMJ*, Vol. 318, 1999, pp. 846–850.

Davis, Lisa, Ronald P. Vega, and Jeffrey McLeod, "Additional Descriptive Analyses and Future Directions," in Lisa Davis, Amanda Grifka, Kristin Williams, and Margaret Coffey, eds., *2016 Workplace and Gender Relations Survey of Active Duty Members*, OPA Report No. 2016-050, Alexandria, Va.: Office of People Analytics, U.S. Department of Defense, May 2017, pp. 355–453.

Defense Manpower Data Center, *2010 Workplace and Gender Relations Survey of Active Duty Members: Overview Report on Sexual Assault*, DMDC Report No. 2010-025, Washington, D.C., 2011.

———, "Survey Note No. 2013-007: 2012 Workplace and Gender Relations Survey of Active Duty Members," Washington, D.C., March 15, 2013a. As of September 4, 2018: http://www.sapr.mil/public/docs/research/2012_Workplace_and_Gender_Relations_Survey_of_Active_Duty_Members-Survey_Note_and_Briefing.pdf

———, *2012 Workplace and Gender Relations Survey of Active Duty Members: Tabulations of Responses*, DMDC Report No. 2012-065, Washington, D.C., April 2013b. As of September 4, 2018: http://www.sapr.mil/public/docs/research/WGR_ActiveDuty_2012_Report.pdf

DMDC—*See* Defense Manpower Data Center.

Elliott, D. M., D. S. Mok, and J. Briere, "Adult Sexual Assault: Prevalence, Symptomatology, and Sex Differences in the General Population," *Journal of Traumatic Stress*, Vol. 17, No. 3, June 2004, pp. 203–211.

Ellsberg, M., Diana J. Arango, Matthew Morton, Floriza Gennari, Sveinung Kiplesund, Manuel Contreras, and Charlotte Watts, "Prevention of Violence Against Women and Girls: What Does the Evidence Say?" *The Lancet*, Vol. 385, No. 9977, April 18, 2015, pp. 1555–1566.

Farris, Coreen, Lisa H. Jaycox, Terry L. Schell, Amy E. Street, Dean G. Kilpatrick, and Terri Tanielian, "Sexual Harassment and Gender Discrimination Findings: Active Component," in Andrew R. Morral, Kristie L. Gore, and Terry L. Schell, eds., *Sexual Assault and Sexual Harassment in the U.S. Military: Volume 2. Estimates for Department of Defense Service Members from the 2014 RAND Military Workplace Study*, Santa Monica, Calif.: RAND Corporation, RR-870/2-1-OSD, 2015, pp. 31–54. As of September 4, 2018: https://www.rand.org/pubs/research_reports/RR870z2-1.html

Fitzgerald, L. F., F. Drasgow, C. L. Hulin, M. J. Gelfand, and V. J. Magley, "Antecedents and Consequences of Sexual Harassment in Organizations: A Test of an Integrated Model," *Journal of Applied Psychology*, Vol. 82, 1997, pp. 578–589.

Fitzgerald, L. F., F. Drasgow, and V. J. Magley, "Sexual Harassment in the Armed Forces: A Test of the Integrated Model," *Military Psychology*, Vol. 11, No. 3, 1999, pp. 329–343.

Gidycz, C. A., C. N. Coble, L. Latham, and M. J. Layman, "Sexual Assault Experience in Adulthood and Prior Victimization Experiences: A Prospective Analysis," *Psychology of Women Quarterly*, Vol. 17, No. 2, 1993, pp. 151–168.

Gidycz, Christine A., John R. McNamara, and Katie M. Edwards, "Women's Risk Perception and Sexual Victimization: A Review of the Literature," *Aggression and Violent Behavior*, Vol. 11, No. 5, 2006, pp. 441–456.

Gilmore, A. K., M. A. Lewis, and W. H. George, "A Randomized Controlled Trial Targeting Alcohol Use and Sexual Assault Risk Among College Women at High Risk for Victimization," *Behavioral Research and Therapy*, Vol. 74, November 2015, pp. 38–49.

Ghosh-Dastidar, Bonnie, Terry L. Schell, and Andrew R. Morral, "Analytic Methods," in Andrew R. Morral, Kristie L. Gore, and Terry L. Schell, eds., *Sexual Assault and Sexual Harassment in the U.S. Military: Volume 1. Design of the 2014 RAND Military Workplace Study*, Santa Monica, Calif.: RAND Corporation, RR-870/1-OSD, 2014, pp. 57–64. As of September 4, 2018: https://www.rand.org/pubs/research_reports/RR870z1.html

Ghosh-Dastidar, Bonnie, Terry L. Schell, Andrew R. Morral, and Marc N. Elliott, "The Efficacy of Sampling Weights for Correcting Non-Response Bias," in Andrew R. Morral, Kristie L. Gore, and Terry L. Schell, eds., *Sexual Assault and Sexual Harassment in the U.S. Military: Volume 4. Investigations of Potential Bias in Estimates from the 2014 RAND Military Workplace Study*, Santa Monica, Calif.: RAND Corporation, 2015, RR-870/6-OSD, pp. 21–70. As of September 4, 2018: https://www.rand.org/pubs/research_reports/RR870z6.html

Harned, Melanie S., Alayne J. Ormerod, Patrick A. Palmieri, Linda L. Collinsworth, and Maggie Reed, "Sexual Assault and Other Types of Sexual Harassment by Workplace Personnel: A Comparison of Antecedents and Consequences," *Journal of Occupational Health Psychology*, Vol. 7, No. 2, April 2002, pp. 174–188.

Humphrey, John A., and Jacquelyn W. White, "Women's Vulnerability to Sexual Assault from Adolescence to Young Adulthood," *Journal of Adolescent Health*, Vol. 27, No. 6, 2000, pp. 419–424.

Jaycox, Lisa H., Terry L. Schell, Andrew R. Morral, Amy Street, Coreen Farris, Dean Kilpatrick, and Terri Tanielian, "Sexual Assault Findings: Active Component," in Andrew R. Morral, Kristie L. Gore, and Terry L. Schell, eds., *Sexual Assault and Sexual Harassment in the U.S. Military: Volume 2. Estimates for Department of Defense Service Members from the 2014 RAND Military Workplace Study*, Santa Monica, Calif.: RAND Corporation, RR-870/2-1-OSD, 2015, pp. 9–30. As of September 4, 2018: https://www.rand.org/pubs/research_reports/RR870z2-1.html

Kalof, L., K. K. Eby, J. L. Matheson, and R. J. Kroska, "The Influence of Race and Gender on Student Self-Reports of Sexual Harassment by College Professors," *Gender and Society*, Vol. 15, No. 2, April 2001, pp. 282–302.

Kessler, Ronald, *Behavioral-Based Predictors of Workplace Violence in the Army STARRS*, Boston, Mass.: Harvard Medical School, October 2014. As of September 4, 2018: http://www.dtic.mil/dtic/tr/fulltext/u2/a610948.pdf

Kiely, Michele, Ayman A. E. El-Mohandes, M. Nabil El-Khorazaty, and Marie G. Gantz, "An Integrated Intervention to Reduce Intimate Partner Violence in Pregnancy: A Randomized Trial," *Obstetrics and Gynecology*, Vol. 115, No. 2, February 2010, pp. 273–283.

Kilpatrick, Dean G., Ron Acierno, Heidi S. Resnick, Benjamin E. Saunders, and Connie L. Best, "A 2 Year Longitudinal Analysis of the Relationships Between Violent Assault and Substance Use in Women," *Journal of Consulting and Clinical Psychology*, Vol. 65, No. 5, October 1997, pp. 834–847.

Kilpatrick, Dean G., Heidi S. Resnick, Kenneth J. Ruggiero, Lauren M. Conoscenti, and Jenna Mccauley, *Drug-Facilitated, Incapacitated, and Forcible Rape: A National Study*, Charleston, S.C.: Medical University of South Carolina, National Crime Victims Research and Treatment Center, February 1, 2007.

Kimerling, Rachel, Kristian Gima, Mark W. Smith, Amy Street, and Susan Frayne, "The Veterans Health Administration and Military Sexual Trauma," *American Journal of Public Health*, Vol. 97, No. 12, 2007, pp. 2160–2166.

Lalor, Kevin, and Rosaleen McElvaney, "Child Sexual Abuse, Links to Later Sexual Exploitation/ High-Risk Sexual Behavior, and Prevention/Treatment Programs," *Trauma, Violence, and Abuse*, Vol. 11, No. 4, 2010, pp. 159–177.

Larimer, Mary E., Amy R. Lydum, Britt K. Anderson, and Aaron P. Turner, "Male and Female Recipients of Unwanted Sexual Contact in a College Student Sample: Prevalence Rates, Alcohol Use, and Depression Symptoms," *Sex Roles*, Vol. 40, No. 3–4, 1999, pp. 295–308.

LeardMann, C. A., A. Pietrucha, K. M. Magruder, B. Smith, M. Murdoch, I. G. Jacobson, M. A. Ryan, G. Gackstetter, T. C. Smith, and Millennium Cohort Study Team, "Combat Deployment Is Associated with Sexual Harassment or Sexual Assault in a Large, Female Military Cohort," *Women's Health Issues*, Vol. 23, No. 4, 2013, pp. e215–e223.

Littleton, Heather, Danny Axsom, and Amie Grills-Taquechel, "Sexual Assault Victims' Acknowledgment Status and Revictimization Risk," *Psychology of Women Quarterly*, Vol. 33, No. 1, 2009, pp. 34–42.

Martindale, M., "Sexual Harassment in the Military," *Sociological Practice Review*, Vol. 2, 1991, pp. 200–216.

Marx, Brian P., Victoria Van Wie, and Alan M. Gross, "Date Rape Risk Factors: A Review and Methodological Critique of the Literature," *Aggression and Violent Behavior*, Vol. 1, No. 1, 1996, pp. 27–45.

McDonald, P., "Workplace Sexual Harassment 30 Years On: A Review of the Literature," *International Journal of Management Reviews*, Vol. 14, No. 1, 2012, pp. 1–17.

McMullin, Darcy, and Jacquelyn W. White, "Long-Term Effects of Labeling a Rape Experience," *Psychology of Women Quarterly*, Vol. 30, No. 1, 2006, pp. 96–105.

Merrill, Lex L., Carol E. Newell, Cynthia J. Thomsen, Steven R. Gold, Joel S. Milner, Mary P. Koss, and Sandra G. Rosswork, "Childhood Abuse and Sexual Revictimization in a Female Navy Recruit Sample," *Journal of Traumatic Stress*, Vol. 12, No. 2, April 1999, pp. 211–225.

Messman-Moore, T. L., A. L. Brown, and L. E. Koelsch, "Posttraumatic Symptoms and Self-Dysfunction as Consequences and Predictors of Sexual Revictimization," *Journal of Traumatic Stress*, Vol. 18, No. 3, 2005, pp. 253–261.

Messman-Moore, T. L., and P. J. Long, "Child Sexual Abuse and Revictimization in the Form of Adult Sexual Abuse, Adult Physical Abuse, and Adult Psychological Maltreatment," *Journal of Interpersonal Violence*, Vol. 15, No. 5, May 2000, pp. 489–502.

Michael, Robert T., John H. Gagnon, Edward O. Lauman, and Gina Kolata, *Sex in America: A Definitive Survey*, New York: Warner Books, 1994.

Mohler-Kuo, Meichun, George W. Dowdall, Mary P. Koss, and Henry Wechsler, "Correlates of Rape While Intoxicated in a National Sample of College Women," *Journal of Studies on Alcohol*, Vol. 65, No. 1, 2004, pp. 37–45.

Morral, Andrew R., Kristie L. Gore, and Terry L. Schell, eds., *Sexual Assault and Sexual Harassment in the U.S. Military: Volume 1. Design of the 2014 RAND Military Workplace Study*, Santa Monica, Calif.: RAND Corporation, RR-870/1-OSD, 2014. As of September 4, 2018:
https://www.rand.org/pubs/research_reports/RR870z1.html

————, eds., *Sexual Assault and Sexual Harassment in the U.S. Military: Volume 2. Estimates for Department of Defense Service Members from the 2014 RAND Military Workplace Study*, Santa Monica, Calif.: RAND Corporation, RR-870/2-1-OSD, 2015a. As of September 4, 2018: https://www.rand.org/pubs/research_reports/RR870z2-1.html

————, eds., *Sexual Assault and Sexual Harassment in the U.S. Military: Volume 3. Estimates for United States Coast Guard Members from the 2014 RAND Military Workplace Study*, Santa Monica, Calif.: RAND Corporation, RR-870/3-1-OSD, 2015b. As of September 4, 2018: https://www.rand.org/pubs/research_reports/RR870z4.html

————, eds., *Sexual Assault and Sexual Harassment in the U.S. Military: Volume 4. Investigations of Potential Bias in Estimates from the 2014 RAND Military Workplace Study*, Santa Monica, Calif.: RAND Corporation, RR-870/6-OSD, 2016. As of September 4, 2018: https://www.rand.org/pubs/research_reports/RR870z6.html

Morral, Andrew R., Terry L. Schell, Matthew Cefalu, Jessica Hwang, and Andrew Gelman, *Sexual Assault and Sexual Harassment in the U.S. Military:* Volume 5. Estimates for Installation- and Command-Level Risk of Sexual Assault and Sexual Harassment from the 2014 RAND Military Workplace Study, Santa Monica, Calif.: RAND Corporation, RR-870/7-OSD, 2018. As of September 30, 2018: https://www.rand.org/pubs/research_reports/RR870z7.html

National Defense Research Institute, *Sexual Assault and Sexual Harassment in the U.S. Military: Top-Line Estimates for Active-Duty Service Members from the 2014 RAND Military Workplace Study*, Santa Monica, Calif.: RAND Corporation, RR-870-OSD, 2014. As of September 4, 2018: https://www.rand.org/pubs/research_reports/RR870.html

Norris, J., P. S. Nurius, and L. A. Dimeff, "Through Her Eyes: Factors Affecting Women's Perception of and Resistance to Acquaintance Sexual Aggression Threat," *Psychology of Women Quarterly*, Vol. 20, No. 1, 1996, pp. 123-145.

Roodman, A. A., and A. Clum, "Revictimization Rates and Method Variance: A Meta-Analysis," *Clinical Psychology Review*, Vol. 21, 2001, pp. 183-204.

Rothman, Emily F., Deinera Exner, and Allyson L. Baughman, "The Prevalence of Sexual Assault Against People Who Identify as Gay, Lesbian, or Bisexual in the United States: A Systematic Review," *Trauma, Violence, and Abuse*, Vol. 12, No. 2, 2011, pp. 55–66.

Sadler, Anne G., Brenda M. Booth, Brian L. Cook, and Bradley N. Doebbeling, "Factors Associated with Women's Risk of Rape in the Military Environment," *American Journal of Industrial Medicine*, Vol. 43, No. 3, 2003, pp, 262–273.

Schell, Terry L., and Andrew R. Morral, "Branch of Service Differences in the Rates of Sexual Assault and Sexual Harassment," in Andrew R. Morral, Kristie L. Gore, and Terry L. Schell, eds., *Sexual Assault and Sexual Harassment in the U.S. Military: Volume 2. Estimates for Department of Defense Service Members from the 2014 RAND Military Workplace Study*, Santa Monica, Calif.: RAND Corporation, RR-870/2-1-OSD, 2015a, pp. 61–76. As of September 4, 2018: https://www.rand.org/pubs/research_reports/RR870z2-1.html

————, "Findings from the Reserve Component," in Andrew R. Morral, Kristie L. Gore, and Terry L. Schell, eds., *Sexual Assault and Sexual Harassment in the U.S. Military: Volume 2. Estimates for Department of Defense Service Members from the 2014 RAND Military Workplace Study*, Santa Monica, Calif.: RAND Corporation, RR-870/2-1-OSD, 2015b, pp. 77–87. As of September 4, 2018: https://www.rand.org/pubs/research_reports/RR870z2-1.html

Schry, A. R., and S. W. White, "Sexual Assertiveness Mediates the Effect of Social Anxiety on Sexual Victimization Risk on College Women," *Behavior Therapy*, Vol. 44, No. 1, March 2013, pp. 125–136.

Single, Eric, and Scot Wortley, "Drinking in Various Settings as It Relates to Demographic Variables and Level of Consumption: Findings from a National Survey in Canada," *Journal of Studies on Alcohol*, Vol. 54, No. 5, 1993, pp. 590–599.

Stockdale, M. S., M. Visio, and L. Batra, "The Sexual Harassment of Men: Evidence for a Broader Theory of Sexual Harassment and Sex Discrimination," *Psychology, Public Policy, and Law*, Vol. 5, No. 3, 1999, pp. 630–664.

Street, Amy E., Jaimie L. Gradus, Jane Stafford, and Kacie Kelly, "Gender Differences in Experiences of Sexual Harassment: Data from a Male-Dominated Environment," *Journal of Consulting and Clinical Psychology*, Vol. 75, No. 3, June 2007, pp. 464–474.

Street, Amy E., Anthony J. Rosellini, Robert J. Ursano, Steven G. Heeringa, Eric D. Hill, John Monahan, James A. Naifeh, Maria V. Petukhova, Ben Y. Reis, Nancy A. Sampson, Paul D. Bliese, Murray B. Stein, Alan M. Zaslavsky, and Ronald C. Kessler, "Developing a Risk Model to Target High-Risk Preventive Interventions for Sexual Assault Victimization Among Female US Army Soldiers," *Clinical Psychological Science*, Vol. 4, No. 6, 2016, pp. 939–956.

Street, Amy E., Jane Stafford, Clare M. Mahan, and Ann Hendricks, "Sexual Harassment and Assault Experienced by Reservists During Military Service: Prevalence and Health Correlates," *Journal of Rehabilitation Research and Development*, Vol. 45, No. 3, 2008, pp. 409–419.

Tabachnick, B. G., and L. S. Fidell, *Using Multivariate Statistics*, New York: Pearson Education, 2007.

Testa, Maria, and Jennifer A. Livingston, "Alcohol Consumption and Women's Vulnerability to Sexual Victimization: Can Reducing Women's Drinking Prevent Rape?" *Substance Use and Misuse*, Vol. 44, No. 9–10, 2009, pp. 1349–1376.

Tjaden, Patricia, and Nancy Thoennes, *Prevalence, Incidence, and Consequences of Violence Against Women: Findings from the National Violence Against Women Survey*, Research in Brief, Washington, D.C.: National Institute of Justice and Centers for Disease Control and Prevention, NCJ 172837, November 1998.

Tjur, Tue, "Coefficients of Determination in Logistic Regression Models—A New Proposal: The Coefficient of Discrimination," *American Statistician*, Vol. 63, No. 4, 2009, pp. 366–372.

Turchik, Jessica A., and Susan M. Wilson, "Sexual Assault in the U.S. Military: A Review of the Literature and Recommendations for the Future," *Aggression and Violent Behavior*, Vol. 15, No. 4, 2010, pp. 267–277.

Ullman, Sarah E., "A Critical Review of Field Studies on the Link of Alcohol and Adult Sexual Assault in Women," *Aggression and Violent Behavior*, Vol. 8, No. 5, 2003, pp. 471–486.

U.S. Department of Defense, Safe Helpline, website, undated. As of September 4, 2018:
https://www.rainn.org/dod-safe-helpline

———, *2014–2016 Sexual Assault Prevention Strategy*, Washington, D.C., April 30, 2014. As of August 10, 2017:
http://sapr.mil/public/docs/prevention/DoD_SAPR_Prevention_Strategy_2014-2016.pdf

———, "DoD Launches Online Learning Program to Help Military Survivors of Sexual Assault," press release, Washington, D.C., June 12, 2017. As of August 8, 2017:
https://www.defense.gov/News/News-Releases/News-Release-View/Article/1211427/
dod-launches-online-learning-program-to-help-military-survivors-of-sexual-assau/

U.S. Merit Systems Protection Board, *Sexual Harassment in the Federal Workplace: Trends, Progress, Continuing Challenges*, Washington, D.C., 1995.

Vogler, Roger E., "What College Students Need to Know About Drinking," *Journal of Alcohol and Drug Education*, Vol. 39, No. 3, 1994, pp. 99–112.

Willness, C. R., P. Steel, and K. Lee, "A Meta-Analysis of the Antecedents and Consequences of Workplace Sexual Harassment," *Personnel Psychology*, Vol. 60, No. 1, 2007, pp. 127–162.

Wilson, A. E., K. S. Calhoun, and J. A. Bernat, "Risk Recognition and Trauma-Related Symptoms Among Sexually Revictimized Women," *Journal of Consulting and Clinical Psychology*, Vol. 67, No. 5, 1999, pp. 705–710.

Yeater, Elizabeth A., and William O'Donohue, "Sexual Assault Prevention Programs: Current Issues, Future Directions, and the Potential Efficacy of Interventions with Women," *Clinical Psychology Review*, Vol. 19, No. 7, November 1999, pp. 739–771.

Zou, G., "A Modified Poisson Regression Approach to Prospective Studies with Binary Data," *American Journal of Epidemiology*, Vol. 159, No. 7, 2004, pp. 702–706.